AF409611

CRAZY DUMPLINGS

AMANDA ROBERTS

© 2014 Amanda Roberts
www.AmandaRobertsWrites.com

Cover design & other images © 2014 Cherith Vaughan
www.shreddedpotato.com

All rights reserved. No part of this publication may be reproduced or transmitted in any form or by any means, electronic or mechanical, including photocopying, recording, or any information storage or retrieval system, without express written permission from the publisher.

ALSO BY AMANDA ROBERTS

Fiction

Threads of Silk

The Man in the Dragon Mask

The Qing Dynasty Mysteries

Murder in the Forbidden City

Murder in the British Quarter

Murder at the Peking Opera

The Touching Time Series

The Emperor's Seal

The Empress's Dagger

The Slave's Necklace

Nonfiction

The Crazy Dumplings Cookbook

Crazy Dumplings II: Even Dumplinger

For Seth, my gracious guinea pig.

CONTENTS

PART II

DUMPLINGS: THE PERFECT VEHICLES FOR LEFTOVERS

PART III
SWEET DUMPLINGS

PART IV
SAUCES

PART V
METRIC CONVERSIONS

INTRODUCTION

Dumplings. Wontons. *Jiaozi*. This remarkably simple food is found throughout Asia and in Chinese restaurants and kitchens around the world. But have you ever filled a dumpling wrapper with chicken? Cheese? Refried beans? Hardly anyone has! I decided to write this fun cookbook to show the many crazy things you can stuff in a dumpling wrapper for an easy meal or snack.

When I moved to China in 2010, I was already known for being a pretty good cook; I loved to cook things from scratch and my brownies were famous. I also loved Chinese food, so when my husband and I talked about moving to China, food was one of our least pressing concerns.

It ended up being one of our biggest issues.

Our first home was in a little country town of a million people (yeah, I know that means a "city" the size of San Francisco in the U.S., but in China, that is just a small town with few conveniences). There was no Walmart or McDonald's or a Chinese equivalent. At the only supermarket, there were no canned or prepared foods (no canned beans, canned tomatoes, or mac and cheese), and the only frozen foods you could find were dumplings (good-bye Lean Cuisines!). Forget chicken breasts, you could only buy whole chickens (with the head still attached!). The only milk available was sterilized, which tastes disgusting (like it's already gone sour) and has no health benefits. There was no cheese, no cream, and no butter.

When it came to my new kitchen, I was at a total loss. I couldn't even turn on the stove. It had an external gas tank (which was empty) and a battery to ignite the flame (which was dead). There was no oven; Chinese households don't have ovens. The only faucet in the whole house with hot water was the shower, so even washing dishes was a difficult process.

Then, of course, was the fact that we were in Hunan, one of the two provinces in China known for spicy food (the other being Sichuan). Now, I thought I liked spicy food. I like hot salsa and would go for the red end of the sauce pool at Buffalo Wild Wings. But the American idea of spicy can't even begin to compare to Hunan spicy. I quickly learned to say "bu yao la," ("I don't want it spicy"), but many times restaurants, especially small ones, didn't have non-spicy options. They just looked at me like I was crazy. Even if I went to a nicer restaurant and asked for "whatever you have that is not spicy," it would come out swimming in peppers. So even though cooking at home meant completely relearning how to cook, it ended up being the only option to starving since restaurant food was too hot.

I've now been living in China for four years. Even though that first year in the middle of nowhere (or as locals call it "the middle of the middle of nowhere") was one of the most difficult of our lives, my husband and I are grateful for the experience. It made us stronger, heartier, and proved that we are survivors who can overcome great odds. I'm not saying that China is some great, uncivilized backwater and we are amazing people for daring to live there, but I have a much better understanding of and sympathy for anyone who immigrates to a new country. We are now in a new, modern city with a Sam's Club, Ikea, and more Western restaurants than we can count, but I still use the skills I learned from living without Western food or conveniences on a daily basis.

This book was not written specifically for people living overseas, but I did keep them in mind. I tried to use as many "from scratch" recipes as possible, using ingredients that should be easy to find at any local grocery store, whether that store is in Warrensburg, Missouri or Lixian, Hunan. However, there are several recipes that use cheese and milk since many of my readers are in Western countries and procuring these items is not a hardship. There are also several vegetarian recipes, or they could be made vegetarian by leaving the meat out or substituting it for a soy product.

The biggest thing I want readers to take away from this book is to learn to be adaptable. You don't have to make any of these recipes exactly the way I have them described here. Use what you have and make changes where necessary to make these dumplings your own.

COOKING NOTES

Servings

All of the following recipes are for 12 dumplings, which is just about perfect for a dinner for two. You can easily double or triple the ingredients to make large quantities of dumplings for families or get-togethers. You can also make smaller dumplings (only ½ inch in diameter dough balls) as hors d'oeuvres for parties.

Dumpling Wrappers

In America and China, dumplings have become so popular that the wrappers can easily be bought already prepared. While these can significantly cut down your cooking time, I prefer making my own because they are thicker and I think they taste better. Even in China, every time we go to restaurants that are "famous for their dumplings," what usually sets their dumplings apart is homemade dumpling wrappers.

Cooking Time

The cooking time for all of these recipes is about 45-60 minutes depending on how you cook your dumplings. While mixing the flour and water to make the dumplings doesn't take long, you have to wait

15 minutes for the dough to set up. Rolling out the dough takes another 15 minutes. Frying the dumplings takes about 5 minutes, but boiling or steaming them takes about another 10 minutes. Of course, if you use commercial dumpling wrappers, this time is significantly reduced.

The Wok

It is easiest to fry a dumpling in a wok. The round shape and even cooking temperature of a wok make it perfect for creating golden brown dumplings. Carbon steel woks are the best as they heat and cool quickly. If you use a gas range, you can use a round or flat bottom wok; if you use an electric range, you will want a flat bottom wok. Both conduct heat evenly, but a round bottom wok will redirect too much heat back to the range on an electric stove and can damage the heating elements.

Cooking

Almost all of the recipes in the book are for fried dumplings. Fried dumplings tend to taste the best, look the best, and have the best texture. However, many can also be steamed or boiled if you prefer the taste or want to cut out a few calories. Here are the three ways you can cook your dumplings:

1. To fry dumplings, preheat 1 cup of oil for 30 seconds on high heat, then lower heat to medium. Cook dumplings on each side for about 3 minutes or until golden brown.
2. To steam dumplings, place in a steamer basket or on an elevated plate in a wok over water on high heat for about 10 minutes.
3. To boil dumplings, place in boiling water for about 10 minutes.
4. Always cut a dumpling open and check to make sure it is cooked through, especially when using a meat filling.

Freezing and Leftovers

Once you prepare the dumplings, but before you cook them, they can be frozen and kept for several weeks. Place the prepared dumplings on a cookie sheet and put them into the freezer for 15 minutes. Then, put the frozen dumplings into a freezer bag and place them back into the freezer. When cooking the frozen dumplings, do not thaw but cook immediately. Preparing large batches of dumplings is a great weekend activity for families so they can then have pre-made, but homemade, snacks ready to go for the kids all week or as emergency dinner ideas.

Cooked leftover dumplings can be refrigerated for a day or two and reheated in an oven at 350 degrees for 10 minutes.

Filling Ingredients

To help make my instructions more succinct, many times I will say something like "add all filling ingredients." Typically, this will mean everything listed except the dumpling wrappers, frying oil, and dipping sauces, unless otherwise noted.

Also, many of the ingredients need to be chopped, minced, diced, or finely sliced small enough that the ingredients can be mixed together. I simplified the directions for these ingredients as "chopped," but however you slice or dice it, make sure that you are able to get a little of everything in each dumpling.

FOLDING DUMPLINGS

I will be the first to admit that I am terrible at folding dumplings. I'm not an artist, so making lovely folds and artistic designs just isn't in me. For me, a "dumplinger" (a little plastic tool for folding and crimping dumplings) is the best way for me to fold dumplings. However, there are a few easy folds that even I can do and have illustrated for you below.

The Simple Fold

The Pyramid

The Loop

You can find lots more examples of folded dumplings on my

Pinterest page (http://www.pinterest.com/amandachina/crazy-dumplings/). Feel free to experiment with your own dumpling folding styles and be sure to send me pictures!

BASIC DUMPLING WRAPPER

This recipe is for making 12 dumpling wrappers, enough for all the dumpling filling recipes in this book. Keep some extra flour on hand for flouring the counter and your hands to keep everything from sticking. Also, feel free to add more flour if necessary if the dough is too sticky.

- 3/4 cup flour
- 1/3 cup boiling water
- Dash of salt
- Flour for dusting

1. Mix flour and salt together.
2. Slowly drizzle in water, mixing with a chopstick or fork.
3. Leave in the bowl, covered with plastic wrap, for 15 minutes.
4. Gather dough up into a ball and knead for a minute or two until the dough is smooth.
5. Pinch off a small portion of dough and roll into a ball about 1 inch in diameter. Roll out into a flat circle on the counter, dusting with flour to keep dough from sticking.

6. Choose a dumpling filling from elsewhere in this book and continue following the directions there.

PART I

SAVORY DUMPLINGS

TRADITIONAL DUMPLING FILLING

Fresh ginger has a very strong taste. The last thing you want to do is bite into a chunk of fresh ginger! I always use a microplane to shred the ginger as small as possible. I use a garlic press to get the most flavor out of fresh garlic.

- 1 cup ground meat (beef, pork, or turkey)
- 1 tsp ginger, microplaned
- 1 garlic clove, pressed
- 1 Tbsp green onions, chopped
- 12 dumpling wrappers
- 1 cup of oil, if frying
- Soy Sauce, Thai Sweet Chili Sauce, or Chinese Chili Sauce (See recipes in the Sauces section)

1. Mix meat and spices together.
2. Spoon mixture into dumpling wrappers and pinch closed.
3. Cook dumplings.
4. To fry dumplings, preheat oil for 30 seconds on high heat,

then lower heat to medium. Cook dumplings on each side for about 3 minutes or until golden brown.

5. To steam dumplings, place in a steamer basket or on an elevated plate in a wok over water on high heat for about 10 minutes.

6. To boil dumplings, place in boiling water for about 10 minutes.

7. Always cut a dumpling open to make sure it is cooked through.

8. Serve hot with soy sauce, Thai Sweet Chili Sauce, or Chinese Chili Sauce for dipping.

SICHUAN CRAWFISH DUMPLINGS

This recipe was requested by Kickstarter backer Greg Leuch. Sichuan peppercorns are spicy and can be an acquired taste, but they are truly unique. I don't know how easy it is to get Sichuan peppercorns in the West, but they are most likely available at Asian import stores. They can also be purchased online. Try buying whole peppercorns, putting them in a hand grinder, and keeping it close by your stove to add a hit of spice to whatever you might cook up.

- 2 Tbsp oil
- 1 cup crawfish (or prawn) meat, chopped
- ¼ cup corn kernels
- ¼ cup onion, chopped
- 1 tsp ginger, microplaned
- 1 garlic clove, pressed
- 1 tsp Sichuan peppercorns, ground
- 1 tsp Chinese 5 spice powder
- dash of salt
- 12 dumpling wrappers

- 1 cup oil for frying
- Chinese Chili Sauce for dipping (see recipe in the Sauces section)

1. In a wok, heat 2 Tbsp oil. Add all the filling ingredients. Stir-fry until meat is cooked and onion is tender. Remove mixture from heat and let it cool before handling.
2. Spoon mixture into dumpling wrappers and pinch closed.
3. To fry dumplings, preheat oil for 30 seconds on high heat, then lower heat to medium. Cook dumplings on each side for about 3 minutes or until golden brown.
4. Serve hot with Chinese Chili Sauce for dipping.

CRUNCHY CRAWFISH DUMPLINGS

This recipe was suggested by Kickstarter backer Stephen Lato. These make good breakfast dumplings and can be steamed or fried.

- 2 eggs
- ½ cup milk
- ½ cup flour
- 1 Tbsp creole seasoning
- 1 cup crawfish or prawn meat
- 1 cup oil
- ¼ cup onion, chopped
- ¼ cup mushrooms, chopped
- 2 Tbsp oil
- 12 dumpling wrappers
- 1 cup oil for frying

1. In one bowl, mix milk and 1 egg together. In another bowl, combine flour and creole seasoning.

2. Coat the crawfish meat in the flour. Dip coated crayfish into the egg wash. Recoat the crawfish with the flour mix.
3. In a wok, heat 1 cup of oil. Carefully add the crawfish one at a time and deep-fry each piece for about 2 minutes, or until golden brown. Chop fried crawfish and set aside.
4. In a wok, heat 2 Tbsp oil. Sauté onion and mushrooms until tender. Add chopped crayfish and stir. Add in other egg and scramble mixture. Remove mixture from heat and let cool before handling.
5. Spoon mixture into dumpling wrappers and pinch closed.
6. To fry dumplings, preheat oil for 30 seconds on high heat, then lower heat to medium. Cook dumplings on each side for about 3 minutes or until golden brown.
7. To steam dumplings, place in a steamer basket or on an elevated plate in a wok over water on high heat for about 10 minutes.

XIAOLONGBAO DUMPLINGS

In my experience, xiaolongbao (also known as "soup dumplings") are made in baozi wrappers (steamed buns), not dumpling wrappers. This might because baozi's are sturdier and can hold in the liquid filling better. But Kickstarter backer Mark Henderson said he had xiaolongbao as a dumpling in Beijing, so why not? You will just want to make sure the dumplings are closed tight so the filling doesn't spill out. Also, I am parting from tradition with regards to the filling. The soup part of xiaolongbao is usually made with gelled broth. I don't know how common broth jelly is in the West, but it is very time-consuming to make. It can also be difficult to get the consistency right. So we are going to take regular chicken broth and freeze it. You'll just have to work fast to get the dumplings made before it melts.

- ½ cup ground pork
- ½ cup raw shrimp, chopped
- 2 Tbsp soy sauce
- 1 Tbsp Shaoxing wine
- 2 tsp sugar
- 1 tsp ginger, finely grated
- dash of salt
- dash of pepper

- ½ cup chicken broth
- 12 dumpling wrappers
- 1 cup oil for frying

1. Combine all the filling ingredients and blend well. Place filling in the freezer overnight (at least 8 hours).
2. Once filling is frozen, spoon mixture into dumpling wrappers and pinch closed.
3. To fry dumplings, preheat oil for 30 seconds on high heat, then lower heat to medium. Cook dumplings on each side for about 3 minutes or until golden brown.
4. To steam dumplings, place in a steamer basket or on an elevated plate in a wok over water on high heat for about 10 minutes.
5. Be sure to cut a dumpling open to make sure they are cooked through.
6. Be careful when you bite into the dumplings because the melted broth might spill out.

HUNAN-STYLE SPICY PORK DUMPLINGS

Kickstarter backer and Crazy Dumpling *artist Cherith and I lived in the same city in Hunan for over a year. She took to the spicy food there better than I ever did, but this one is a favorite for both of us. The great thing about cooking this at home is being able to control the heat level. Most restaurants in Hunan don't really have "bu yao la" ("not spicy") options, which is one of the main reasons I became so passionate about cooking at home after moving abroad.*

- 5 dried red chilies (feel free to add more if you like it Hunan spicy!)
- 1 Tbsp Shaoxing wine
- 1 Tbsp soy sauce
- 2 tsp cornstarch
- 1 cup ground pork
- 1 tsp ginger, microplaned
- 1 garlic clove, pressed
- 2 green onions, chopped
- 2 tsp chili oil (feel free to add more if you like it Hunan spicy!)

- 1 Tbsp cumin
- Dash of black pepper
- 12 dumpling wrappers
- 1 cup oil for frying
- Soy sauce, Chinese Chili Sauce, or Thai Sweet Chili Sauce for dipping (see recipe in the Sauces section)

1. Place dried red chilies in a bowl of warm water for 20 minutes to soften. Remove from water and finely chop.
2. In a bowl, whisk together wine, soy sauce, and cornstarch. Blend well with all other filling ingredients.
3. Spoon mixture into dumpling wrappers and pinch closed.
4. To fry dumplings, preheat oil for 30 seconds on high heat, then lower heat to medium. Cook dumplings on each side for about 3 minutes or until golden brown.
5. Be sure to cut a dumpling open to make sure they are cooked through.
6. Serve hot with soy sauce, Chinese Chili Sauce, or Thai Sweet Chili Sauce.

SHRIMP AND PORK FUN GOR

*Fun gor is actually a dim sum type dumpling, which is usually made with
a thin, translucent rice dumpling wrapper. But we are going to make them
with jiaozi wrappers because we can. Thanks to Michael R. Ward, a
Kickstarter backer, for requesting this recipe!*

- 1 tsp cornstarch
- 1 Tbsp chicken broth
- ½ cup ground pork
- ½ cup shrimp, shelled, deveined, chopped
- ¼ cup shitake mushrooms, chopped
- ¼ cup carrot, chopped
- ¼ cup celery, chopped
- ¼ cup peanuts, crushed (optional)
- 2 Tbsp cilantro, chopped
- 1 Tbsp soy sauce
- 1 tsp brown sugar
- 1 tsp hoisin sauce
- 12 dumpling wrappers
- 1 cup oil for frying

- Chinese Chili Sauce for dipping (see recipe in the Sauces
  section)

1. Whisk together cornstarch and chicken broth. Mix
   together with all other filling ingredients.
2. Spoon mixture into dumpling wrappers and pinch closed.
3. To fry dumplings, preheat oil for 30 seconds on high heat,
   then lower heat to medium. Cook dumplings on each side
   for about 3 minutes or until golden brown.
4. To steam dumplings, place in a steamer basket or on an
   elevated plate in a wok over water on high heat for about
   10 minutes.
5. Be sure to cut a dumpling open to make sure they are
   cooked through.
6. Serve hot with Chinese Chili Sauce.

PEKING DUCK DUMPLINGS

Kickstarter backer James McKendrew said I had to include a duck recipe. Here I adapted a traditional Peking duck recipe for dumplings. Peking duck is most famous for its crispy skin and golden brown color, which are achieved through a very complicated preparation process that, ideally, can take days. If you are interested in making your own Peking duck, there are many great recipes available online. Just one cup of leftover duck meat is all you need for this recipe. However, in this recipe, I just went for flavor, not texture or appearance since it is stuffed into a dumpling wrapper and you won't notice the difference, so it tastes like Peking duck, but doesn't have the crispy skin and can be made about an hour. I'm not sure how readily available duck meat is in America, but in China, it is available everywhere.

- ½ cup oyster sauce or hoisin sauce
- 4 Tbsp honey
- 1 tsp Chinese five spice powder
- 1 cup duck meat
- ¼ cup cucumber, chopped
- ¼ cup carrot, chopped
- 1 green onion, chopped

- 12 dumpling wrappers
- 1 cup oil for frying

1. Mix oyster sauce/hoisin sauce, honey, and Chinese five spice powder together. Set aside.
2. Rinse off duck with cold water and pat dry with a paper towel. Slather with half of the sauce mixture.
3. Place the duck in a metal baking dish (if the duck has skin, place it skin side up) and bake at 450 degrees for 30 minutes.
4. When the duck is done, finely chop the meat, including the skin. Mix the duck meat, cucumber, carrot, green onion, and 1 tablespoon of the sauce mix together. Spoon mixture into dumpling wrappers and pinch closed.
5. To fry dumplings, preheat oil for 30 seconds on high heat, then lower heat to medium. Cook dumplings on each side for about 3 minutes or until golden brown.
6. Serve hot with remaining sauce mixture for dipping.

HONEY PEAR DUCK DUMPLINGS

Kickstarter backer Jason Tubbs requested something with duck and pears. I hope he also likes honey.

- 1 cup cooked duck meat, finely chopped
- 2 Tbsp honey
- 1 Tbsp melted butter
- 1 pear, chopped
- 1 tsp parsley, chopped
- dash of salt
- 12 dumpling wrappers
- 1 cup oil for frying

1. Mix all the filling ingredients. Blend well.
2. Spoon mixture into dumpling wrappers and pinch closed.
3. To fry dumplings, preheat oil for 30 seconds on high heat, then lower heat to medium. Cook dumplings on each side for about 3 minutes or until golden brown.

ASIAN SHORT RIB DUMPLINGS

Of course, you don't want bones in your dumplings, so using actual short ribs would not be suitable for this recipe. But Asian short ribs are delicious, and Kickstarter backer Margaret Sherman really wanted them included in the book. If you are able to find boneless short ribs, awesome, but if you can't, you can also use boneless beef tips.

- ¼ cup soy sauce
- 2 Tbsp vinegar
- 1 garlic clove, pressed
- 1 lemongrass stalk, outer husk removed, chopped and smashed
- 1 tsp ginger, microplaned
- 2 Tbsp brown sugar
- 1 green onion, chopped
- 1 tsp cayenne pepper
- 2 Tbsp hoisin sauce
- juice of 1 orange
- juice of 1 lemon
- 1 cup rib meat (or similar cut), chopped
- 12 dumpling wrappers

- 1 cup oil for frying

1. In a wok, add all the ingredients except the rib meat. Bring the sauce to a boil.
2. Reduce heat and add meat. Simmer until meat is cooked through. Drain sauce and set aside. Let meat cool before handling.
3. Spoon meat mixture into dumpling wrappers and pinch closed.
4. To fry dumplings, preheat oil for 30 seconds on high heat, then lower heat to medium. Cook dumplings on each side for about 3 minutes or until golden brown.
5. Be sure to cut a dumpling open to make sure they are cooked through.
6. Serve with reserved sauce for dipping.

KOREAN MANDU DUMPLINGS

Kickstarter backer Candace Fetzer requested these Korean mandu dumplings. They are similar to Chinese dumplings, but they have cabbage and tofu mixed in. They are typically served with kimchee. I didn't include a kimchee recipe because even though kimchee isn't particularly difficult to make, it is extremely time-consuming, which clashes with the quick and easy theme of this book. Mandus are also typically served with a spicy chili sauce, so pair them with the Chinese Chili Sauce recipe that can be found in the Sauces section of this book.

- ½ cup ground beef
- 2 green onions, chopped
- ½ cup cabbage, chopped
- ¼ cup bean sprouts, chopped
- ¼ cup firm tofu, chopped
- 1 Tbsp hoisin sauce
- 1 tsp salt
- 1 tsp black pepper
- 12 dumpling wrappers
- 1 cup oil for frying

- Chinese Chili Sauce for dipping (see recipe in the Sauces section)

1. Mix all of the filling ingredients together.
2. Spoon mixture into dumpling wrappers and pinch closed.
3. To fry dumplings, preheat oil for 30 seconds on high heat, then lower heat to medium. Cook dumplings on each side for about 3 minutes or until golden brown.
4. Be sure to cut a dumpling open to make sure they are cooked through.
5. Serve hot with Chinese Chili Sauce for dipping and a side of kimchee.

POKÉMON DUMPLINGS

Kickstarter backer Jasmine Fellows loves dumplings as much as I do. For a long time, she kept the blog Jasmine Dumplings. *This is a recipe adapted from her blog that she modified from the Nintendo DS game,* Cooking Guide.

no Pokémon fainted during the testing of this recipe.

- 1 cup ground Pokémon meat (or any ground meat)
- ¼ cup onion, chopped
- 1 tsp ginger, microplaned
- 1 Tbsp sesame oil
- 1 Tbsp soy sauce
- ½ Tbsp Shaoxing wine
- 2 Tbsp water
- 1 Tbsp chicken bouillon
- 12 dumpling wrappers
- 1 cup oil for frying
- Soy Sauce, Thai Sweet Chili Sauce, or Chinese Chili Sauce (see recipes in the Sauces section)

1. Mix all of the filling ingredients together.
2. Spoon mixture into dumpling wrappers and pinch closed.
3. To fry dumplings, preheat oil for 30 seconds on high heat, then lower heat to medium. Cook dumplings on each side for about 3 minutes or until golden brown.
4. Be sure to cut a dumpling open to make sure they are cooked through.
5. Serve hot with sauces for dipping.

THAI PEANUT STIR-FRY DUMPLINGS

This was made for Kickstarter backer Jay Haney, who wanted something peanutty and vegetarian. This recipe is really versatile. You can use whatever veggies you like; the ones listed here are just examples. You could even use frozen mixed vegetables and just mash them a bit or chop them up smaller after they cook. All the ingredients have to be chopped up really small to get a little bite of everything in each dumpling.

- ½ cup vegetable broth
- 1 Tbsp cornstarch
- ¼ cup peanut butter
- 1 Tbsp soy sauce
- 1 Tbsp honey
- 1 Tbsp brown sugar
- 1 tsp sesame oil
- 1 tsp ginger, microplaned
- 1 Tbsp chili garlic sauce
- 2 cloves garlic, pressed
- 2 Tbsp vegetable oil
- 2 cups chopped vegetables (onion, broccoli florets, carrots, peas, mushrooms, eggplant, etc.)

- ½ cup water
- 12 dumpling wrappers
- 1 cup oil for frying

1. In a saucepan, whisk cornstarch into vegetable broth. Add peanut butter, soy sauce, honey, brown sugar, sesame oil, ginger, garlic, and chili garlic sauce and mix well. Bring sauce to a boil over medium heat, stirring continuously. Turn heat to low and keep stirring until sauce thickens. Remove from heat and set aside.
2. In a wok, heat 2 Tbsp vegetable oil on medium heat. Add vegetables and water and cover. Let veggies steam until tender, about 5 minutes. Remove veggies from heat, drain off any liquid, and let cool before handling.
3. Mix cooked veggies and 2 Tbsp of the sauce mixture together in a bowl.
4. Spoon veggie mixture into dumpling wrappers and pinch closed.
5. To fry dumplings, preheat oil for 30 seconds on high heat, then lower heat to medium. Cook dumplings on each side for about 3 minutes or until golden brown.
6. Serve hot with remaining sauce mixture.

THAI YUM NUAH BEEF DUMPLINGS

*This recipe was requested by Kickstarter backer Kathleen Doerr.
Technically, Thai yum nuah is a salad, but when the ingredients are finely
chopped, they stuff into a dumpling wrapper just fine!*

- ¼ cup cilantro, chopped
- Juice of 2 limes
- 2 Tbsp fish sauce (hoisin sauce is a good substitute)
- 1 Tbsp brown sugar
- 1 jalapeno pepper, chopped, seeds removed for less heat
- 1 cup boneless steak, cooked as desired and chopped (this
  is a great way to use that leftover steak from a previous
  dinner)
- 1 tomato, chopped (peeled and seeds removed)
- ¼ cup cucumber, chopped
- ¼ cup red onion, chopped
- ¼ cup celery, chopped
- 12 dumpling wrappers
- 1 cup oil for frying
- Thai Sweet Chili Sauce for dipping (see recipe in the
  Sauces section)

1. In a bowl, mix cilantro, lime juice, fish sauce, and brown sugar. Mix well until sugar is dissolved. Set aside.
2. Mix remaining filling ingredients. Pour fish sauce mixture over beef mixture and blend well.
3. Spoon mixture into dumpling wrappers and pinch closed.
4. To fry dumplings, preheat oil for 30 seconds on high heat, then lower heat to medium. Cook dumplings on each side for about 3 minutes or until golden brown.
5. Serve hot with Thai Sweet Chili Sauce for dipping.

ROASTED VEGGIE DUMPLINGS

This dumpling filling has a delicious flavor, thanks to roasting the veggies beforehand. Roasting does take longer than stir-frying, but it is definitely worth it.

- 4 Tbsp oil
- 1 garlic clove, pressed
- 1 Tbsp fresh parsley leaves, chopped
- 1 green onion, chopped
- 1 Tbsp salt
- ½ cup cherry tomatoes, chopped
- ½ cup eggplant, chopped
- ½ cup zucchini, chopped
- ½ cup fresh corn kernels
- ¼ cup parmesan cheese, shredded (optional)
- 12 dumpling wrappers
- 1 cup oil for frying

1. Preheat oven to 350 degrees.

2. In a bowl, combine 4 Tbsp of oil, garlic, parsley chives, and salt and blend well. Add vegetables to the oil and toss well to coat.

3. On a baking sheet, spread the vegetables evenly in a single layer. Make sure the eggplant is skin side down. Roast for about 20 minutes until all veggies are tender. Remove from the oven and let cool before handling. Remove eggplant meat from skins and then mix all the veggies together. Toss with parmesan cheese if using.

4. Spoon veggie mixture into dumpling wrappers and pinch closed.

5. To fry dumplings, preheat oil for 30 seconds on high heat, then lower heat to medium. Cook dumplings on each side for about 3 minutes or until golden brown.

EGGPLANT PARMESAN DUMPLINGS

Thanks to Heather L. Whittaker, a Kickstarter backer, for requesting this vegetarian recipe.

- 2 Tbsp Marinara Sauce (see recipe in the Sauces section)
- 1 cup eggplant, chopped
- 1 Tbsp Italian seasoning
- 1 garlic clove, pressed
- 1 tsp onion powder
- ¼ cup mozzarella, shredded
- ¼ cup parmesan cheese
- dash of salt
- 12 dumpling wrappers
- 1 cup oil for frying
- Extra Marinara Sauce for dipping (see recipe in the Sauces section)

1. Mix together all the filling ingredients and blend well.

2. Spoon mixture into dumpling wrappers and pinch closed.
3. To fry dumplings, preheat oil for 30 seconds on high heat, then lower heat to medium. Cook dumplings on each side for about 3 minutes or until golden brown.
4. Serve with additional Marinara Sauce for dipping.

MUSHROOM AND RICOTTA DUMPLINGS

Who needs meat? This is such a delicious vegetarian option, you won't even miss it!

- 1 cup ricotta cheese
- ½ cup mushrooms, chopped
- Juice and zest of 1 lemon
- Dash of salt
- Dash of black pepper
- Dash of cayenne pepper
- 2 green onions, chopped
- 2 Tbsp Italian seasoning
- 1 garlic clove, pressed
- 12 dumpling wrappers
- 1 cup oil for frying
- Marinara Sauce for dipping (see recipe in the Sauces section)

1. Mix all filling ingredients.

2. Spoon mixture into dumpling wrappers and pinch closed.
3. To fry dumplings, preheat oil for 30 seconds on high heat, then lower heat to medium. Cook dumplings on each side for about 3 minutes or until golden brown.
4. Serve hot with Marinara Sauce for dipping.

MAPLE PORK AND APPLE DUMPLINGS

This recipe is for Kickstarter backer Jack Oskay who requested something with apples. This is a sweet and savory dish that is perfect for fall weather.

- 2 Tbsp maple syrup
- 1 tsp spicy brown mustard
- dash of salt
- 2 Tbsp breadcrumbs
- 1 cup pork loin cutlets, chopped
- 1 Tbsp apple cider vinegar
- 1 apple, chopped
- 12 dumpling wrappers
- 1 cup oil for frying

1. Combine all ingredients and mix well.
2. Spoon mixture into dumpling wrappers and pinch closed.
3. To fry dumplings, preheat oil for 30 seconds on high heat, then lower heat to medium. Cook dumplings on each side for about 3 minutes or until golden brown.

4. Always cut a dumpling open to make sure it is cooked through.

HERB STUFFING AND PORK CHOP DUMPLINGS

Pork chops with stuffing are one of my easy go-to dinners. Putting the ingredients into a dumpling was a natural evolution of this fun and easy meal. Any brown gravy mix makes a great dipping sauce as well.

- 2 Tbsp oil
- ½ cup boneless pork chop meat, chopped
- 2 Tbsp orange juice
- 2 tsp rosemary
- 1 tsp sage
- 1 garlic clove, pressed
- dash of salt
- ½ cup chicken broth
- ½ cup dried stuffing mix
- 12 dumpling wrappers
- 1 cup oil for frying

1. In a wok, heat 2 Tbsp oil. Add meat and stir-fry until

cooked through. Add orange juice, rosemary, sage, garlic, salt, and broth. Mix well and heat to a boil.

2. Add stuffing crumbs and toss until broth is absorbed. Remove from heat and let cool.
3. Spoon mixture into dumpling wrappers and pinch closed.
4. To fry dumplings, preheat oil for 30 seconds on high heat, then lower heat to medium. Cook dumplings on each side for about 3 minutes or until golden brown.
5. Always cut a dumpling open to make sure it is cooked through.

FANCY LOBSTER DUMPLINGS

I can't kill anything. Except spiders. Kill them all. But I could never kill a lobster (they're kind of cute). This is a great way to use the less expensive frozen lobster tails you can find in almost any supermarket and still sound like you are fancy schmancy by serving a lobster-based dish at dinner or at a potluck.

- ½ cup cooked lobster meat, chopped
- ½ cup breadcrumbs
- 2 green onions, chopped
- juice of 1 lemon
- ½ cup melted butter, divided
- ¼ cup parmesan cheese
- 1 garlic clove, pressed
- 1 Tbsp Italian seasoning
- dash of salt
- 12 dumpling wrappers
- 1 cup oil for frying

1. Mix lobster, breadcrumbs, onions, lemon, ¼ cup melted butter, and cheese.
2. Spoon mixture into dumpling wrappers and pinch closed.
3. To fry dumplings, preheat oil for 30 seconds on high heat, then lower heat to medium. Cook dumplings on each side for about 3 minutes or until golden brown.
4. In another bowl, mix ¼ cup melted butter, garlic, Italian seasoning, and salt. Either pour the butter sauce over the lobster dumplings or use it as a dipping sauce.

AU GRATIN POTATO DUMPLINGS

This recipe is for Kickstarter backer Daniel Lanigan who wanted something with potatoes. I hope he likes potatoes and cheese!

- 1 cup potatoes, chopped
- ¼ cup onion, chopped
- ½ cup shredded cheese
- ¼ cup milk
- 1 Tbsp butter
- dash of salt
- dash of pepper
- 12 dumpling wrappers
- 1 cup oil for frying

1. Combine all filling ingredients and blend well.
2. Spoon mixture into dumpling wrappers and pinch closed.
3. To fry dumplings, preheat oil for 30 seconds on high heat, then lower heat to medium. Cook dumplings on each side for about 3 minutes or until golden brown.

SAUERKRAUT PORK DUMPLINGS

This recipe was requested by Kickstarter backer Mike Pruente Jr. I'm not a sauerkraut expert, but everything I read about it says it takes days to prepare, which doesn't really jive with the quick and easy nature of dumplings. So while most of my recipes use as little prepared food as possible, we are going to take the easy way out here and use jarred sauerkraut (don't hate me).

- 1 cup cooked pork, chopped
- ½ cup sauerkraut
- 1 slice of bacon, fried crispy and chopped
- 1 tsp brown sugar
- 2 Tbsp apple sauce
- 1 tsp thyme
- 1 tsp mustard
- 1 tsp oregano
- 1 tsp paprika
- dash of salt
- dash of pepper
- 12 dumpling wrappers
- 1 cup oil for frying

1. Combine all filling ingredients and blend well.
2. Spoon mixture into dumpling wrappers and pinch closed.
3. To fry dumplings, preheat oil for 30 seconds on high heat, then lower heat to medium. Cook dumplings on each side for about 3 minutes or until golden brown.

LEMONGRASS TOFU DUMPLINGS

This very flavorful vegetarian recipe was inspired by Randy Graham's Lemongrass Tofu recipe he posted on iPinionSyndicate.com. He has lots of great vegetarian recipes on his website valley-vegetarian.com.

- 2 Tbsp oil
- 1 cup firm tofu, chopped
- ½ cup mushrooms, chopped
- 1 Tbsp soy sauce
- 2 Tbsp sugar
- 1 Tbsp hoisin sauce
- 2 green onions, chopped
- ¼ cup onion, chopped
- 1 clove garlic, pressed
- 1 tsp chili oil
- 1 stalk of lemongrass, outer husk removed, chopped and smashed
- 12 dumpling wrappers
- 1 cup oil for frying

1. In a wok, heat 2 Tbsp oil. Add tofu and mushrooms. Stir-fry for about 3 minutes (cooking time may vary depending on the exact tofu used).
2. Add soy sauce, sugar, hoisin sauce, onions, garlic, chili oil, and lemongrass. Stir-fry and mix thoroughly for about 2 minutes. Remove mixture from heat and let cool before handling.
3. Spoon mixture into dumpling wrappers and pinch closed.
4. To fry dumplings, preheat oil for 30 seconds on high heat, then lower heat to medium. Cook dumplings on each side for about 3 minutes or until golden brown.

TACO DUMPLINGS

This is the beginning of my Mexican-inspired dumpling section. One of the things I really miss here in China is Mexican (or Tex-Mex) food, so I have spent a lot of time recreating my favorite Mexican foods, many of which I have adapted into dumplings.

- 1 cup ground meat (beef, pork, or turkey)
- ¼ cup cheese, shredded
- 1 Tbsp chili seasoning
- 1 Tbsp ground cumin
- ½ Tbsp garlic powder
- ½ Tbsp onion powder
- ¼ cup cilantro, finely chopped (optional)
- 12 dumpling wrappers
- 1 cup of oil for frying
- Salsa, Guacamole, cheese sauce, sour cream (all possible optional dips; see recipes in the Sauces section)

1. Mix ground meat, cheese, spices, and cilantro together.

2. Spoon mixture into dumpling wrappers and pinch closed.
3. To fry dumplings, preheat oil for 30 seconds on high heat, then lower heat to medium. Cook dumplings on each side for about 3 minutes or until golden brown.
4. Always cut a dumpling open to make sure it is cooked through.
5. Serve hot with sauces for dipping.

BURRITO DUMPLINGS

Burritos are one of my favorite foods, so I was devastated when I moved to China and canned refried beans were no longer available to me. Thankfully, I discovered that soybeans make a perfect substitute for pinto beans. One can of refried beans is enough for this recipe, or just start with one cup of dry pinto beans or soybeans to make refried beans from scratch!

- 1 cup refried beans
- 1 Tbsp chili seasoning
- 1 Tbsp onion powder
- 1 Tbsp garlic powder
- 1 Tbsp cumin
- 2 Tbsp water
- ¼ cup cheese, shredded
- 12 dumpling wrappers
- 1 cup of oil for frying
- Salsa, Guacamole, cheese sauce, sour cream (all possible optional dips; see recipes in the Sauces section)

1. In a small saucepan, mix beans, spices, and water. Bring to a gentle boil over medium heat, stirring constantly to prevent burning. Add more water if mixture seems too thick.
2. Remove beans from heat and add in cheese. You can use any kind of cheese you want to help make the recipe your own. Cheddar cheese is the old standby, but pepper jack gives it a nice kick!
3. Spoon mixture into dumpling wrappers and pinch closed.
4. To fry dumplings, preheat oil for 30 seconds on high heat, then lower heat to medium. Cook dumplings on each side for about 3 minutes or until golden brown.
5. Serve hot with sauces for dipping.

MEXICAN RICE DUMPLINGS

This recipe is so flavorful, you won't even miss the meat. You'll be lucky if the rice mixture even makes it into a dumpling wrapper because it is also a great side dish on its own.

- 1 cup cooked rice
- ¼ cup cheese, shredded
- ¼ cup Salsa (see recipe in the Sauces section)
- 1 Tbsp chili powder
- 1 Tbsp cumin powder
- ½ Tbsp garlic powder
- ½ Tbsp onion powder
- 12 dumpling wrappers
- 1 cup oil for frying
- Salsa, Guacamole, cheese sauce, sour cream (all possible optional dips; see recipes in the Sauces section)

1. Mix rice, cheese, Salsa, and seasonings.

2. Spoon mixture into dumpling wrappers and pinch closed.
3. To fry dumplings, preheat oil for 30 seconds on high heat, then lower heat to medium. Cook dumplings on each side for about 3 minutes or until golden brown.
4. Serve hot with sauces for dipping.

CHICKEN TAQUITO DUMPLINGS

Chicken taquitos are typically rolled into a corn tortilla and fried, but I prefer flour tortillas to corn tortillas, so I love this version. I recommend a spicy cheese in this recipe.

- 1 cup cooked chicken, chopped
- ¼ cup cheese, shredded
- ¼ cup sweet corn kernels
- ¼ cup canned black beans
- ½ Tbsp cumin
- 1 tsp chipotle powder
- 1 Tbsp fresh cilantro, chopped
- 12 dumpling wrappers
- 1 cup oil for frying
- Salsa, Guacamole, cheese sauce, sour cream (all possible optional dips; see recipe in the Sauces section)

1. Mix chicken, cheese, corn, beans, cumin, chipotle powder, and cilantro.

2. Spoon mixture into dumpling wrappers and pinch closed.
3. To fry dumplings, preheat oil for 30 seconds on high heat, then lower heat to medium. Cook dumplings on each side for about 3 minutes or until golden brown.
4. Serve hot with sauces for dipping.

FAJITA DUMPLINGS

These dumplings have all the flavor and fun of build-it-yourself fajitas with the convenience of dumpling wrappers. These would be excellent for a party with a spread of sauces people can choose from.

- 1 cup cooked chicken or beef, chopped
- ¼ cup cheese, shredded
- ¼ cup bell pepper, chopped
- ¼ cup onion, chopped
- 2 tsp chili powder
- 1 tsp salt
- 1 tsp paprika
- ½ tsp garlic powder
- ¼ tsp cayenne pepper
- ½ tsp cumin
- 12 dumpling wrappers
- 1 cup oil for frying
- Salsa, Guacamole, cheese sauce, sour cream (all possible optional dips; see recipe in the Sauces section)

1. Mix all the filling ingredients.
2. Spoon mixture into dumpling wrappers and pinch closed.
3. To fry dumplings, preheat oil for 30 seconds on high heat, then lower heat to medium. Cook dumplings on each side for about 3 minutes or until golden brown.
4. Serve hot with sauces for dipping.

JALAPEÑO CHEESE DUMPLINGS

This is technically a vegetarian recipe since the bacon bits are optional.

- ¼ cup sugar
- 2 Tbsp water
- ¼ cup grenadine
- ½ cup cheese, shredded
- ¼ cup cream cheese
- 2 Tbsp milk
- ¼ cup jalapeño peppers, minced, seeds removed for less heat
- 1 tsp cumin
- 1 tsp garlic powder
- 1 Tbsp bacon bits (optional)
- 12 dumpling wrappers
- 1 cup oil for frying

1. In a bowl, mix sugar, water, and grenadine. Chill in fridge for an hour
2. In another bowl, mix cheese, cream cheese, milk, peppers, spices, and bacon bits together.
3. Spoon cheese mixture into dumpling wrappers and pinch closed.
4. To fry dumplings, preheat oil for 30 seconds on high heat, then lower heat to medium. Cook dumplings on each side for about 3 minutes or until golden brown.
5. Serve hot with chilled syrup mixture for dipping.

BEEF STIR-FRY DUMPLINGS

*Kickstarter backer Carolyn Brindle requested a beef stir-fry dumpling.
Backer Jonas Claumarch also wanted something with peppers and garlic.
This is easy to fix and any leftovers could be tossed on a bed of rice for an
easy dinner.*

- 1 Tbsp cornstarch
- 1 Tbsp water
- 2 Tbsp soy sauce
- 1 garlic clove, pressed
- 1 Tbsp hoisin sauce
- 1 tsp cayenne pepper
- 2 Tbsp oil
- 1 cup sirloin steak or top round steak, chopped
- ¼ cup carrot, chopped
- ¼ cup bell pepper (any color), chopped
- ¼ cup mushrooms, chopped
- 1 green onion, chopped
- 12 dumpling wrappers
- 1 cup oil for frying

1. In a bowl, whisk together cornstarch, water, soy sauce, garlic, hoisin sauce, and cayenne pepper. Set aside.
2. In a wok, heat 2 Tbsp oil. Add steak and vegetables. Stir-fry until meat is cooked and veggies are tender.
3. Add sauce mixture to meat mixture and blend well. Reduce heat and simmer until sauce thickens. Remove from heat and let the mixture cool before handling.
4. Spoon mixture into dumpling wrappers and pinch closed.
5. To fry dumplings, preheat oil for 30 seconds on high heat, then lower heat to medium. Cook dumplings on each side for about 3 minutes or until golden brown.

CHICKEN SHRIMP SAUSAGE JAMBALAYA DUMPLINGS

These dumplings are packed with flavor and texture thanks to all the different meats inside.

- 2 Tbsp oil
- ¼ cup boneless, skinless chicken breast, chopped
- ¼ cup raw peeled, deveined shrimp, chopped
- ¼ cup Andouille or other smoked sausage, chopped
- ¼ cup onion, chopped
- ¼ cup green bell pepper, chopped
- 1 Tbsp Creole seasoning
- 1 tsp cayenne seasoning
- ¼ cup cooked rice
- 12 dumpling wrappers
- 1 cup oil for frying

1. In a wok, heat 2 Tbsp oil. Add all other filling ingredients (except rice) and stir-fry, stirring continually and pressing with a spatula.

2. Once all meat is cooked and onion and bell pepper are
    soft, add rice. Remove from heat and let cool before
    handling.
3. Spoon mixture into dumpling wrappers and pinch closed.
4. To fry dumplings, preheat oil for 30 seconds on high heat,
    then lower heat to medium. Cook dumplings on each side
    for about 3 minutes or until golden brown.

SPICY MOROCCAN SALMON DUMPLINGS

This recipe was suggested by Kickstarter backer Stephen Lato. This recipe is spicy and the dumplings can be either fried or steamed.

- 5 dried red chili peppers, seeds removed for less heat
- 1 clove garlic, pressed
- dash of salt
- 1 tsp cumin
- Juice of 1 lemon
- 1 Tbsp oil
- 2 Tbsp oil
- ¼ cup onion, chopped
- ¼ cup celery, chopped
- ¼ cup bell pepper, chopped
- ½ cup smoked salmon, chopped
- 1 egg
- ¼ cup breadcrumbs
- 12 dumpling wrappers
- 1 cup oil for frying

1. Place red peppers in a bowl and cover with hot water for about 20 minutes. Once softened, remove from water.
2. In a blender, combine peppers, garlic, salt, cumin, lemon juice, and 1 Tbsp oil. Set sauce aside.
3. In a wok, heat 2 Tbsp oil. Add onion, celery, and bell pepper and sauté until soft.
4. Add salmon to the wok and sauté for 2 minutes. Add one egg and scramble the mixture. Remove from heat. Fold in breadcrumbs and sauce mixture.
5. Spoon mixture into dumpling wrappers and pinch closed.
6. To fry dumplings, preheat oil for 30 seconds on high heat, then lower heat to medium. Cook dumplings on each side for about 3 minutes or until golden brown.
7. To steam dumplings, place in a steamer basket or on an elevated plate in a wok over water on high heat for about 10 minutes.

SICILIAN SAUSAGE DUMPLINGS

This recipe was suggested by Kickstarter backer Stephen Lato.

- 1 cup ground pork
- ¼ Tbsp whole fennel seeds
- ½ Tbsp black pepper
- 1 tsp salt
- ½ Tbsp paprika
- ¼ Tbsp basil
- ¼ Tbsp oregano
- dash of black pepper
- ½ Tbsp parsley, chopped
- ¼ Tbsp cayenne pepper
- ¼ cup red wine
- 12 dumpling wrappers
- 1 cup oil for frying

1. Combine all filling ingredients and blend well. For best results, refrigerate overnight.

2. When ready to make dumplings, let filling set out for about 30 minutes (this will make the filling more malleable).
3. Spoon mixture into dumpling wrappers and pinch closed.
4. To fry dumplings, preheat oil for 30 seconds on high heat, then lower heat to medium. Cook dumplings on each side for about 3 minutes or until golden brown.

TEALEAVES AND PORK DUMPLINGS

This recipe was suggested by Kickstarter backer The Cleaver Quarterly.

- 2 Tbsp green or oolong tea leaves
- ½ cup boiling water
- 1 cup ground pork
- ¼ cup green chilies, chopped
- 1 green onion, chopped
- 1 garlic clove, pressed
- 1 tsp ginger, microplaned
- 1 Tbsp soy sauce
- 12 dumpling wrappers
- 1 cup oil for frying

1. In a cup, combine the tea and water. Steep the tea for about 2 minutes. Strain out the tea leaves (you can drink the tea if you want).
2. Combine the tea leaves with the rest of the filling ingredients.

3. Spoon mixture into dumpling wrappers and pinch closed.
4. To fry dumplings, preheat oil for 30 seconds on high heat, then lower heat to medium. Cook dumplings on each side for about 3 minutes or until golden brown.
5. Be sure to cut a dumpling open to make sure they are cooked through.

"STUFFED PEPPER" DUMPLINGS

This recipe contains the typical ingredients usually found stuffed in a bell pepper. Here, the bell pepper is chopped up and the whole mixture is stuffed into a dumpling wrapper. How fun is that?

- ¼ cup Marinara Sauce (see recipe in the Sauces section)
- 1 tsp cumin
- 2 Tbsp oil
- ½ cup ground chicken or pork
- ¼ cup bell pepper, chopped
- ¼ cup zucchini, chopped
- ¼ cup onion, chopped
- ¼ cup cooked rice
- 12 dumpling wrappers
- 1 cup oil for frying

1. In a bowl, combine Marinara Sauce and cumin. Set aside.
2. In a wok, heat up 2 Tbsp oil. Add meat, bell pepper, zucchini, and onion. Stir-fry until meat is cooked and

veggies are tender. Remove from heat. Add rice and 2
Tbsp of sauce.

3. Spoon mixture into dumpling wrappers and pinch closed.
4. To fry dumplings, preheat oil for 30 seconds on high heat,
   then lower heat to medium. Cook dumplings on each side
   for about 3 minutes or until golden brown.
5. Serve with extra Marinara Sauce for dipping.

"STUFFED MUSHROOM" DUMPLINGS

Similar to the "stuffed pepper" dumplings, these aren't actually stuffed mushrooms, but use stuffed mushroom ingredients as the dumpling filling.

- 1 Tbsp oil
- 1 cup mushrooms, chopped
- 1 green onion, chopped
- 1 garlic clove, pressed
- 1 Tbsp Worcestershire sauce
- 4 oz cream cheese, softened
- ¼ cup parmesan cheese
- dash of salt
- dash of pepper
- 1 tsp cayenne pepper
- ¼ cup breadcrumbs
- 12 dumpling wrappers
- 1 cup oil for frying

1. In a wok, heat up 1 Tbsp oil. Add mushrooms, onions,

garlic, and Worcestershire sauce. Sauté until all moisture has evaporated. Set mixture aside and let it cool before continuing.

2. Add cream cheese, parmesan cheese, breadcrumbs, salt, pepper, and cayenne pepper to the mushroom mix.
3. Spoon mixture into dumpling wrappers and pinch closed.
4. To fry dumplings, preheat oil for 30 seconds on high heat, then lower heat to medium. Cook dumplings on each side for about 3 minutes or until golden brown.

PIZZA DUMPLINGS

These are the best for families and large groups because everyone can make their own dumpling filling with the ingredients they want. When I was a kid, my family would do this with "pizza subs" (pizza toppings on French submarine rolls). Now, in my own family, we have exchanged the French rolls for Chinese dumpling wrappers.

- 1 jar pizza sauce
- ½ Tbsp of Italian seasoning
- ½ Tbsp garlic powder
- Dash of salt
- 12 pepperoni, chopped (optional)
- 1 cup mozzarella cheese, shredded
- ½ cup chopped "toppings:" black olives, green olives, onion, bell pepper, mushrooms, anchovies, etc.
- 12 dumpling wrappers
- 1 cup of oil for frying

1. Mix pizza sauce, Italian seasoning, garlic powder, and salt

in a saucepan and cook over medium heat until the sauce boils. Remove from heat.

2. Mix pepperoni, cheese, toppings, and 2 tablespoons of the pizza sauce mixture together.

3. Spoon cheese mixture into wrappers and pinch closed.

4. To fry dumplings, preheat oil for 30 seconds on high heat, then lower heat to medium. Cook dumplings on each side for about 3 minutes or until golden brown.

5. Serve hot with remaining pizza sauce for dipping.

SWEET AND SOUR CHICKEN DUMPLINGS

This sweet and sour chicken recipe calls for canned pineapple. You could use fresh pineapple, but you might not get as much juice to use in the sauce.

- 2 Tbsp oil
- 1 cup boneless, skinless chicken breast, chopped
- ¼ cup bell pepper, chopped
- ¼ cup carrot, chopped
- ¼ cup onion, chopped
- ¼ cup canned pineapple, chopped
- 4 Tbsp pineapple juice, divided
- 12 dumpling wrappers
- 1 cup of oil for frying
- Sweet and Sour Sauce for dipping (see recipe in the Sauces section)

1. In a wok, heat 2 Tbsp oil. Add chicken, vegetables,

pineapple, and 2 Tbsp pineapple juice. Sauté until chicken is cooked and veggies are tender. Remove from heat and let cool before handling.

2. Add 2 Tbsp pineapple juice.

3. Spoon mixture into wrappers and pinch closed.

4. To fry dumplings, preheat oil for 30 seconds on high heat, then lower heat to medium. Cook dumplings on each side for about 3 minutes or until golden brown.

5. Always cut a dumpling open to make sure it is cooked through.

6. Serve with Sweet and Sour Sauce for dipping.

ORANGE CHICKEN DUMPLINGS

After sweet and sour chicken, orange chicken is probably most people's favorite. I couldn't put one in a dumpling and not the other.

- 1 Tbsp oil
- 2 cloves of garlic, pressed
- 1 tsp ginger, microplaned
- 1 tsp cayenne pepper
- 1 Tbsp soy sauce
- 2 Tbsp sugar
- Juice and zest of two oranges
- 2 tsp cornstarch
- 1 cup cooked chicken, chopped
- 1 green onion, chopped (for garnish, optional)
- 1 Tbsp toasted sesame seeds (for garnish, optional)
- 12 dumpling wrappers
- 1 cup of oil for frying

1. In a wok, heat 1 Tbsp oil. Add garlic and ginger. Sauté for

about 30 seconds. Add cayenne pepper, soy sauce, and sugar. Stir until sugar is dissolved.

2. Whisk together orange juice and cornstarch. Pour the juice/cornstarch mixture into the sugar mixture. Bring the sauce to a boil. Lower heat to medium and simmer for about one minute. Remove mixture from heat and set aside.
3. Mix chicken and 2 Tbsp of orange mixture.
4. Spoon chicken mixture into wrappers and pinch closed.
5. To fry dumplings, preheat oil for 30 seconds on high heat, then lower heat to medium. Cook dumplings on each side for about 3 minutes or until golden brown.
6. Once dumplings are done, pour the rest of the orange mixture over the dumplings and garnish with onion, sesame seeds, and orange zest.

TERIYAKI DUMPLINGS

I didn't call this "teriyaki chicken" or "teriyaki salmon" because the star of this recipe is the homemade teriyaki sauce. You can use this with almost any filling - chicken, steak, salmon, firm tofu, a vegetable medley, really whatever you want to include. Just substitute the "1 cup of chicken or steak" with whatever kind of filling you want.

- 1 cup cooked chicken or steak, chopped
- 1 Tbsp cornstarch
- 1 Tbsp water
- ½ cup sugar
- ½ cup soy sauce
- ¼ cup apple cider vinegar
- ¼ tsp garlic powder
- ½ tsp ginger powder
- ¼ tsp black pepper
- 12 dumpling wrappers
- 1 cup of oil for frying

1. Add cornstarch, water, soy sauce, vinegar, and seasonings together in a wok and simmer over medium heat until sauce bubbles. Remove from heat and set aside.
2. Mix meat and 2 tablespoons of teriyaki sauce together.
3. Spoon mixture into wrappers and pinch closed.
4. To fry dumplings, preheat oil for 30 seconds on high heat, then lower heat to medium. Cook dumplings on each side for about 3 minutes or until golden brown.
5. Serve hot with remainder of teriyaki sauce for dipping.

RICOTTA ITALIANA DUMPLINGS

One of the proudest moments on my journey of learning to cook overseas was when I learned to make my own spaghetti sauce from scratch. It is hard and takes a lot of time, but it was very gratifying to learn how to make such an amazing sauce myself. While it is easy to just used jarred spaghetti sauce in this recipe, check out my Marinara Sauce recipe in the Sauces section and give it a try at least once!

- 8 oz ricotta cheese
- ½ cup mozzarella cheese, shredded
- 1 Tbsp Italian seasoning
- 1 tsp garlic powder
- 1 tsp onion powder
- 12 dumpling wrappers
- 1 cup of oil for frying
- 1 cup Marinara Sauce (see recipe in the Sauces section)
- Grated parmesan cheese (optional, for garnish)

1. Mix cheeses and seasonings.

2. Spoon mixture into wrappers and pinch closed.
3. To fry dumplings, preheat oil for 30 seconds on high heat, then lower heat to medium. Cook dumplings on each side for about 3 minutes or until golden brown. Set dumplings aside.
4. In a saucepan, bring Marinara Sauce to a boil. Boil for about a minute and then remove from heat.
5. Pour sauce over dumplings. Dust dumplings with parmesan cheese and serve.

ITALIAN SAUSAGE DUMPLINGS

These dumplings are mostly meat, but since you can use sweet or spicy sausage (or a mix of both), they are sure to please almost everyone.

- 1 cup hot or sweet Italian sausage, casings removed, chopped
- ¼ cup carrot, chopped
- ¼ cup celery, chopped
- ¼ cup onion, chopped
- 2 Tbsp oil
- 2 garlic cloves, pressed
- 1 tsp Italian seasoning
- 1 tsp cayenne pepper
- ¼ cup parmesan cheese
- 12 dumpling wrappers
- 1 cup oil for frying
- Marinara Sauce for dipping (see recipe in the Sauces section)

1. Heat oil in a wok. Add sausage and brown. Add veggies, garlic, Italian seasoning, and pepper. Sauté until veggies are tender. Remove from heat and toss with cheese.
2. Spoon mixture into wrappers and pinch closed.
3. To fry dumplings, preheat oil for 30 seconds on high heat, then lower heat to medium. Cook dumplings on each side for about 3 minutes or until golden brown.
4. Serve with Marinara Sauce for dipping.

OMELET DUMPLINGS

Kickstarter backer David Spaxman requested a breakfast dumpling. This dumpling certainly fits that ticket. This breakfast dumpling has very little egg in it to keep it from being too runny and spilling out when you try to fill the dumpling wrapper.

- 1 egg
- ¼ cup cheese, shredded
- 1 cup of vegetables, chopped: onion, bell pepper, mushrooms, avocado, etc.
- ¼ cup cooked ground sausage (or a soy substitute)
- 12 dumpling wrappers
- 1 cup of oil for frying
- Salsa for dipping (see recipe in the Sauces section)

1. Mix egg, cheese, vegetables, and sausage.
2. Spoon mixture into wrappers and pinch closed.
3. To fry dumplings, preheat oil for 30 seconds on high heat,

then lower heat to medium. Cook dumplings on each side for about 3 minutes or until golden brown.

4. Always cut a dumpling open to make sure it is cooked through.

5. Serve with Salsa for dipping.

SWEDISH MEATBALLS WITH GRAVY DUMPLINGS

This recipe was requested by Kickstarter backer Joseph Seliga. I'm not sure why I didn't think of it myself; I love Swedish meatballs! In addition to the meatball gravy, try serving these with a dollop of lingonberry jam, cranberry sauce, or the Strawberry Onion Jam that is in the Sauces section.

- 1 Tbsp unsalted butter
- 2 Tbsp flour
- 1 cup beef broth
- ¼ cup sour cream
- ½ pound ground pork
- ½ pound ground beef
- ¼ cup onion, chopped
- ¼ cup breadcrumbs
- 1 egg yolk
- ¼ cup milk
- 1 tsp parsley
- 1 tsp Worcestershire sauce
- 1 tsp salt
- dash of black pepper
- 12 dumpling wrappers

- 1 cup of oil for frying

1. In a wok, melt butter. Whisk in flour until lightly browned. Gradually whisk in beef broth and cook, whisking constantly, until slightly thickened, about 1-2 minutes. Stir in sour cream. Remove gravy from heat and set aside.
2. In a large bowl, combine beef, pork, onion, breadcrumbs, egg, milk, parsley, Worcestershire sauce, salt, and pepper. Mix well.
3. Spoon mixture into wrappers and pinch closed.
4. To fry dumplings, preheat oil for 30 seconds on high heat, then lower heat to medium. Cook dumplings on each side for about 3 minutes or until golden brown.
5. Always cut a dumpling open to make sure it is cooked through.
6. Serve with gravy for dipping.

CHICKEN CURRY DUMPLINGS

Okay, full disclosure – I hate curry. A large reason for this is I hate coconut and most curry is made with coconut milk, but even when made with regular milk, I still hate curry. However, my husband and all of our British friends love it, so I actually like making curry dumplings for large groups because it means there are plenty of other people around to eat them and leave no leftovers! Kickstarter backer Michael Otto also wanted to see a curry recipe here so I included this for him as well. Feel free to use your favorite curry sauce recipe or mix to make the dumplings your own!

- 1 Tbsp curry powder
- 1 cup coconut milk
- 1 cup chicken breast, chopped
- 1 potato, chopped
- ¼ cup onion, chopped
- 12 dumpling wrappers
- 1 cup of oil for frying

1. Heat coconut milk in a saucepan until boiling. Whisk in

curry powder until dissolved. Bring sauce to a boil, then remove from heat. Set aside.

2. In a small saucepan, boil chicken, potato, and onion until chicken is cooked through and potato is soft. Drain and set aside to cool before handling. Add 2 Tbsp of curry sauce to chicken mixture and blend well.

3. Spoon mixture into wrappers and pinch closed.

4. To fry dumplings, preheat oil for 30 seconds on high heat, then lower heat to medium. Cook dumplings on each side for about 3 minutes or until golden brown.

5. Serve with extra curry sauce for dipping.

HAWAIIAN CHICKEN CURRY DUMPLINGS

This recipe was requested by Zachary Bledsoe, a Kickstarter backer. It's based on a recipe from a popular Honolulu restaurant. Apparently, it's the optional "toppings" that make it really special. I've included these toppings as optional filling ingredients.

- 3 Tbsp butter
- ¼ cup onion, chopped
- 1 garlic clove, pressed
- 1 tsp ginger, microplaned
- 1 Tbsp curry powder
- 1 tsp sugar
- Dash of salt
- 1 cup coconut milk
- 1 cooked chicken breast, chopped
- ½ cup (total) of any of the following optional ingredients: mango chutney, bacon, shredded coconut, chopped peanuts, raisins, chopped hardboiled egg, sweet pickle relish, sliced green onions
- 12 dumpling wrappers
- 1 cup oil for frying

1. In a wok, melt the butter. Add the onion, garlic, and ginger and sauté until onion is tender.
2. Stir in curry powder, sugar, and salt. Slowly pour in coconut milk, stirring constantly. Reduce heat and simmer for 20 minutes. Remove from heat and set aside.
3. Mix chicken breast and any optional ingredients. Add 2 Tbsp of the curry sauce.
4. Spoon chicken mixture into wrappers and pinch closed.
5. To fry dumplings, preheat oil for 30 seconds on high heat, then lower heat to medium. Cook dumplings on each side for about 3 minutes or until golden brown.
6. Serve with extra curry sauce for dipping.

BBQ DUMPLINGS

Be sure to use your favorite BBQ sauce and favorite meat in this recipe to make it your own. I know Kickstarter backer Chris Edwards will want pulled pork in his!

- 1 cup thinly sliced roasted turkey meat, pulled pork, ground beef, etc.
- ½ cup smoked cheese, shredded
- 2 Tbsp BBQ sauce
- 12 dumpling wrappers
- 1 cup of oil for frying
- Extra BBQ sauce for dipping

1. Mix the meat, cheese, and 2 Tbsp BBQ sauce together.
2. Spoon mixture into wrappers and pinch closed.
3. To fry dumplings, preheat oil for 30 seconds on high heat,

then lower heat to medium. Cook dumplings on each side for about 3 minutes or until golden brown.

4. Serve hot with extra BBQ sauce for dipping.

CREAMY CHICKEN DUMPLINGS

This is one of my favorite recipes in this book (and since I love almost all of them, that is saying a lot!). This is my go-to recipe to impress family and friends with my famous Crazy Dumplings.

- 2 Tbsp oil
- ¼ cup mushrooms, chopped
- ¼ cup onion, chopped
- 1 cup chicken breast, chopped
- 1 can of cream of chicken soup
- ¼ cup milk
- 1 Tbsp garlic powder
- 1 Tbsp Italian seasoning
- 1 Tbsp onion powder
- 12 dumpling wrappers
- 1 cup of oil for frying

1. In a wok, heat 2 Tbsp of oil. Sauté mushrooms and onion until tender. Mix in chicken and cook until chicken is no

longer pink. Set mixture aside and let cool before handling.

2. In a saucepan, add soup, milk, and spices together and heat over medium heat until boiling. Remove from heat.

3. Add 2 Tbsp tablespoons of soup mixture to chicken mixture.

4. Spoon chicken mixture into wrappers and pinch closed.

5. To fry dumplings, preheat oil for 30 seconds on high heat, then lower heat to medium. Cook dumplings on each side for about 3 minutes or until golden brown.

6. Serve hot with extra soup mixture for dipping.

TURKEY-DAY LEFTOVER DUMPLINGS

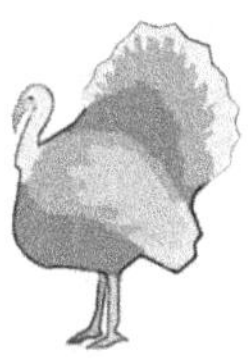

I know lots of people love the "Turkey-Day leftover sandwich," but after three days of sandwiches, they do kind of get old. This is a new, fun way to use up those leftovers.

- 1 cup leftover turkey meat, chopped
- ½ cup leftover stuffing
- ½ cup leftover mashed potatoes
- 1 Tbsp leftover cranberry sauce
- 2 Tbsp leftover turkey gravy
- 12 dumpling wrappers
- 1 cup of oil for frying

1. Mix all of the filling ingredients together.
2. Spoon mixture into wrappers and pinch closed.
3. To fry dumplings, preheat oil for 30 seconds on high heat, then lower heat to medium. Cook dumplings on each side for about 3 minutes or until golden brown.

4. Serve with reheated leftover turkey gravy or cranberry
   sauce (or both) for dipping.

TUNA SALAD DUMPLINGS

*These dumplings are wonderful served with a warm bowl of tomato soup
on a cold day.*

- 1 can of tuna in water, drained
- ½ cup mayonnaise
- 2 Tbsp pickle relish
- 1 Tbsp parmesan cheese
- 1 Tbsp onion, chopped
- 1 Tbsp celery, chopped
- Juice of 1 lemon
- 12 dumpling wrappers
- 1 cup of oil for frying

1. Mix all filling ingredients together.
2. Spoon mixture into wrappers and pinch closed.
3. To fry dumplings, preheat oil for 30 seconds on high heat,
   then lower heat to medium. Cook dumplings on each side
   for about 3 minutes or until golden brown.

BUFFALO WING DUMPLINGS

You can use the Buffalo Sauce in the sauces section of this cookbook or use your own favorite wing sauce to make this recipe your own.

- 1 cup cooked chicken breast, chopped
- ¼ cup celery, chopped
- ¼ cup carrot, chopped
- 2 Tbsp Buffalo Sauce (see recipe in the Sauces section)
- 2 Tbsp blue cheese, crumbled
- 12 dumpling wrappers
- 1 cup of oil for frying

1. Mix all the filling ingredients together.
2. Spoon mixture into wrappers and pinch closed.
3. To fry dumplings, preheat oil for 30 seconds on high heat, then lower heat to medium. Cook dumplings on each side for about 3 minutes or until golden brown.
4. Serve with extra Buffalo Sauce for dipping.

LEMON SHRIMP ALFREDO DUMPLINGS

Shrimp scampi meets Alfredo sauce in a dumpling wrapper. So delicious!

- 2 Tbsp butter
- ¼ cup onion, chopped
- 2 garlic cloves, pressed
- ¼ cup mushrooms, chopped
- 1 tsp flour
- dash of salt
- ¼ cup cream
- juice of 1 lemon
- 1 cup shrimp, peeled, deveined, chopped
- ¼ cup parmesan cheese
- 1 Tbsp fresh parsley, chopped (optional for garnish)
- 12 dumpling wrappers
- 1 cup of oil for frying

1. In a wok, melt butter. Add in onion, garlic, and mushrooms. Sauté until veggies are soft.

2. Reduce heat and add in flour and salt. Stir until flour begins to darken. Gradually whisk in cream.
3. Simmer until sauce thickens, stirring frequently, about 5 minutes.
4. Add in lemon juice and shrimp and cook for about 3 minutes, until shrimp is done. Turn off heat and stir in parmesan cheese.
5. Drain the sauce off the shrimp and vegetables and set aside.
6. Spoon shrimp mixture into wrappers and pinch closed.
7. To fry dumplings, preheat oil for 30 seconds on high heat, then lower heat to medium. Cook dumplings on each side for about 3 minutes or until golden brown.
8. Plate the dumplings. Pour leftover Alfredo sauce over them and garnish with parsley.

BROCCOLI CHEESE RICE DUMPLINGS

These go wonderful with the Turkey-Day Leftover Dumplings because broccoli cheese rice casserole is a common side dish in my family on Turkey-Day.

- 1 cup cooked rice
- ½ cup steamed broccoli, chopped
- ¼ cup cheddar cheese, shredded
- 2 Tbsp milk
- 1 tsp garlic powder
- 12 dumpling wrappers
- 1 cup of oil for frying

1. Mix rice, broccoli, cheese, milk, and garlic together.
2. Spoon mixture into wrappers and pinch closed.
3. To fry dumplings, preheat oil for 30 seconds on high heat, then lower heat to medium. Cook dumplings on each side for about 3 minutes or until golden brown.

WONTON SOUP

Use the Traditional Dumpling Filling recipe from the beginning of the Savory Dumplings chapter to make the dumplings for this soup.

- 1 Tbsp oil
- 1 garlic clove, pressed
- 1 Tbsp ginger, microplaned
- 4 green onions, chopped, divided
- 10 cups chicken broth
- ½ cup bok choy, chopped
- ½ cup mushrooms, finely chopped (shitake mushrooms are really nice in this soup, but you can use whatever mushrooms you like)
- 12 traditional dumplings

1. In a wok, heat 1 Tbsp oil. Add the garlic and ginger and sauté for about a minute. Add half of the green onions and the chicken broth and bring to a boil. Reduce heat and let the broth simmer for about 20 minutes.

2. Increase heat so the broth returns to a boil. Add the bok choy and mushrooms and boil for 3 minutes.

3. Slowly (preferably with a slotted spoon to prevent splashing) add in the dumplings. Stir gently until the wontons float and the dumplings are cooked through, about 10 minutes.

CHICKEN NOODLELESS DUMPLING SOUP

Chicken noodle soup is good for the soul. This soup uses dumplings to hold the soup ingredients as a fun twist on this classic food.

- 10 cups chicken broth
- 2 bay leaves
- 1 Tbsp whole peppercorns
- 3 cloves garlic, pressed
- 1 cup raw chicken breast, chopped
- ¼ cup celery, chopped
- ¼ cup carrot, chopped
- ¼ cup mushrooms, chopped
- ¼ cup onion, chopped
- 12 dumpling wrappers

1. In a pot, add chicken broth, bay leaves, peppercorns, and garlic. Bring to a boil. Let simmer for about 20 minutes.
2. While the broth boils, in a bowl, mix together the chicken

and vegetables. Spoon mixture into dumpling wrappers
and pinch to close.

3. Remove bay leaves and peppercorns from broth. Slowly
   add in the dumplings (preferably with a slotted spoon to
   prevent splashing).
4. Boil dumplings until they float and the chicken is
   completely cooked inside, about 10 minutes.
5. Serve hot with crackers.

BISON BALL DUMPLINGS

Kickstarter backer Zachary Brumleve is a Kansan, and as such wanted a recipe featuring the American Plains Bison. I don't know how easy it is to get Bison meat outside of the American West or Mid-west, so you could substitute the ground bison meat with extra lean ground beef.

- 1 cup ground bison meat
- 1 egg
- ¼ cup onion, chopped
- ½ cup breadcrumbs
- 1 Tbsp fresh parsley, chopped
- 1 tsp Italian seasoning
- 1 Tbsp Worcestershire sauce
- ¼ cup bleu cheese, crumbled
- 12 dumpling wrappers
- 1 cup of oil for frying
- 1 cup Tangy Tomato Sauce for dipping (see recipe in the Sauces section)

1. Mix all of the filling ingredients together. Spoon mixture into dumpling wrappers and pinch closed.
2. To fry dumplings, preheat oil for 30 seconds on high heat, then lower heat to medium. Cook dumplings on each side for about 3 minutes or until golden brown.
3. Always cut a dumpling open to make sure they are cooked through.
4. Serve immediately with Tangy Tomato Sauce for dipping.

MOCK FOIE GRAS DUMPLINGS

Real foie gras is very expensive and can be difficult to make. Of course, if you have some foie gras around (maybe bought on that trip to France but you have no idea how to serve it), you can just skip all these steps and put it into a dumpling wrapper! But if real foie gras is a bit too expensive for your taste, give this recipe a try. It goes amazing with the Strawberry Onion Jam recipe found in the Sauces section. Thanks to Michael Salter, a Kickstarter backer, for requesting this dumpling.

- 1 cup poultry liver (it doesn't have to be duck or goose, this recipe is just as good with chicken liver)
- 1 tsp salt
- ½ cup butter, room temperature
- 1 tsp Worcestershire sauce
- Juice of 1 lemon
- ¼ cup onion
- 12 dumpling wrappers
- 1 cup of oil for frying
- Strawberry Onion Jam for dipping (see recipe in the Sauces section)

1. In a small saucepan, cover liver with water and slowly bring to a boil over low heat. Simmer for about 10 minutes. Add salt and then simmer for about 5 minutes more.
2. In a blender or food processor, blend onions as best you can into a pulp. Add Worcestershire sauce and lemon juice and pulse to mix. Add butter and pulse to mix.
3. Add the cooked liver to the mix and thoroughly blend the mixture until smooth.
4. Move the foie gras to a covered bowl and refrigerate for at least an hour so flavors can settle. The foie gras can be refrigerated overnight.
5. When ready, remove foie gras from refrigerator and spoon mixture into dumpling wrappers and pinch closed.
6. To fry dumplings, preheat oil for 30 seconds on high heat, then lower heat to medium. Cook dumplings on each side for about 3 minutes or until golden brown.
7. Serve hot with Strawberry Onion Jam for dipping.

FLORIDA CONCH DUMPLINGS

Even though I live in China, my husband and I consider Florida our "home," so this dumpling is for the Sunshine State. Conch is a type of sea mollusk, similar to oysters and scallops, though not as popular outside of Florida. This recipe also features Florida oranges, Tupelo honey, and key limes, all staples of a Florida cupboard.

- 1 cup conch meat, chopped (can use scallops if conch is not available in your area)
- ½ cup key lime juice, divided (can substitute with regular lime juice)
- 1 Tbsp oil
- ¼ cup onion, chopped
- ¼ cup cilantro, chopped
- 1 Tbsp Tupelo honey (or use your favorite local honey)
- ½ tsp salt
- 1 tsp cayenne pepper
- 1 tsp garlic powder
- 1 tsp Italian seasoning

- 12 dumpling wrappers
- 1 cup of oil for frying

1. Soak the conch meat in ¼ cup lime juice for 10 minutes. Do not skip this step. The lime juice will chemically "cook" the conch meat. After 10 minutes, drain and discard the used lime juice.
2. In a wok, heat 1 Tbsp oil. Sauté conch meat and onions until onion is tender. Remove from heat.
3. Mix the conch and onion together with the rest of the filling ingredients.
4. Spoon mixture into dumpling wrappers and pinch closed.
5. To fry dumplings, preheat oil for 30 seconds on high heat, then lower heat to medium. Cook dumplings on each side for about 3 minutes or until golden brown.
6. Serve hot with Tartar Sauce for dipping (see recipe in the Sauces section).

TIMEY-WIMEY DUMPLINGS

My darling husband insisted on a fish fingers and custard (vanilla pudding, basically, for Americans) dumpling in honor of his favorite show, Dr. Who, but I just couldn't bring myself to do it. Then I found out that custards don't have to be sweet – they can also be savory! Yay! Problem solved. Enjoy these with your favorite companion tonight!

- ½ cup milk
- ½ Tbsp cornstarch
- 1 tsp mustard
- 1 Tbsp mayonnaise
- Juice of 1 lemon
- 1 tsp dill
- Dash of pepper
- 1 tsp onion powder
- Dash of salt
- 1 tsp cayenne pepper
- 1 egg yolk, whisked
- 1 cup cooked white fish, chopped
- ½ cup breadcrumbs
- 12 dumpling wrappers

- 1 cup of oil for frying

1. In a saucepan, whisk together milk and cornstarch. Then, blend in mustard, mayo, lemon juice, and spices. Heat over medium heat, stirring constantly, until mixture starts to boil. Remove from heat.
2. Whisk in egg yolk. Return to low heat and keep stirring until mixture thickens. Remove from heat.
3. Mix in fish and breadcrumbs. Blend well.
4. Spoon mixture into dumpling wrappers and pinch closed.
5. To fry dumplings, preheat oil for 30 seconds on high heat, then lower heat to medium. Cook dumplings on each side for about 3 minutes or until golden brown.

PART II

—————

DUMPLINGS: THE PERFECT VEHICLES FOR LEFTOVERS

Eleanor Erwin, a Kickstarter backer, requested some ideas for making dumplings out of leftovers. It's a bit hard to come up with only one or two dumplings made of leftovers since everyone has different leftovers in their fridge. However, you have seen just how versatile the dumpling wrapper is. With the right combination of ingredients and the right consistency, you can put almost anything into a dumpling wrapper. Even with the suggestions below, pretty much everything is optional or can be substituted by something else. Honestly, the recipes below could have each had their own page in the book because they are just as delicious, but they all also qualify as "leftover dumplings" so they are gathered here for your convenience. Below are a few ideas for combining leftovers into dumplings just to get you started, but I would love to hear what you put into a dumpling wrapper! Visit my website http://www. twoamericansinchina.com/ and share your dumpling ideas!

LEFTOVER VEGGIE ENCHILADA DUMPLINGS

- 1 cup of any leftover veggies you have in the fridge, chopped: mushrooms, chilies, peppers, cauliflower, broccoli, potatoes, sweet potatoes, onion, corn, etc.
- ½ cup cheese, shredded
- 1 Tbsp cumin
- 1 garlic clove, pressed
- dash of salt
- dash of pepper
- 2 Tbsp Salsa (see recipe in the Sauces section)
- 12 dumpling wrappers
- 1 cup of oil for frying

1. Combine all the filling ingredients and blend well.
2. Spoon mixture into dumpling wrappers and pinch closed.
3. To fry dumplings, preheat oil for 30 seconds on high heat, then lower heat to medium. Cook dumplings on each side for about 3 minutes or until golden brown.
4. Serve hot with Salsa for dipping.

LEFTOVER TEX-MEX FISH DUMPLINGS

- 1 cup leftover, cooked, flakey white fish, chopped (tilapia, halibut, sea bass, flounder, etc.)
- 1 Tbsp chili powder
- 1 tsp cumin
- 1 garlic clove, pressed
- 1 jalapeno, chopped (seeds removed for less heat)
- ¼ cup onion, chopped
- ¼ cup cilantro, chopped
- Juice of one lime
- ¼ cup sour cream
- 12 dumpling wrappers
- 1 cup of oil for frying
- Salsa for dipping (see recipe in the Sauces section)

1. Combine all the filling ingredients and blend well.
2. Spoon mixture into dumpling wrappers and pinch closed.
3. To fry dumplings, preheat oil for 30 seconds on high heat,

then lower heat to medium. Cook dumplings on each side for about 3 minutes or until golden brown.

4. Serve hot with Salsa for dipping.

LEFTOVER SHRIMP WITH CHILI DRESSING DUMPLINGS

- 2 Tbsp oil
- ¼ cup onion, chopped
- 1 jalapeno, chopped (seeds removed for less heat)
- 1 tsp ginger, microplaned
- 1 garlic clove, pressed
- 1 tsp cumin
- juice of 1 lime
- dash of salt
- dash of pepper
- 1 cup leftover cooked shrimp, chopped
- 12 dumpling wrappers
- 1 cup of oil for frying
- Thai Sweet Chili Sauce for dipping (see recipe in the Sauces section)

1. Heat 2 Tbsp oil in a wok. Then, add onion, jalapeno, ginger, garlic, cumin, lime, salt, and pepper. Sauté until onion is tender.

2. Add shrimp and toss to coat. Set mixture aside and let it cool.

3. Spoon mixture into dumpling wrappers and pinch closed.

4. To fry dumplings, preheat oil for 30 seconds on high heat, then lower heat to medium. Cook dumplings on each side for about 3 minutes or until golden brown.

5. Serve hot with Thai Sweet Chili Sauce for dipping.

LEFTOVER THAI FISH CAKE DUMPLINGS

- 1 cup leftover, cooked, flakey white fish, chopped (tilapia, halibut, sea bass, flounder, etc.)
- 1 green onion, chopped
- ¼ cup cilantro, chopped
- 1 garlic clove, pressed
- juice of 1 lemon
- dash of salt
- dash of pepper
- ½ cup breadcrumbs
- 1 egg
- 12 dumpling wrappers
- 1 cup of oil for frying
- Tartar Sauce for dipping (see recipe in the Sauces section)

1. Mix all the filling ingredients. Blend well.
2. Spoon mixture into dumpling wrappers and pinch closed.
3. To fry dumplings, preheat oil for 30 seconds on high heat,

then lower heat to medium. Cook dumplings on each side for about 3 minutes or until golden brown.

4. Serve hot with Tartar Sauce for dipping.

LEFTOVER VEGGIE, BEAN, AND RICE DUMPLINGS

- 1 cup cooked rice
- ¼ cup leftover beans (black, pinto, or kidney beans all work)
- ¼ cup cheese, shredded
- ¼ cup zucchini, chopped
- 1 tomato, chopped (peeled, seeds removed)
- 1 egg
- Dash of salt
- Dash of pepper
- 12 dumpling wrappers
- 1 cup of oil for frying

1. Mix all the filling ingredients. Blend well.
2. Spoon mixture into dumpling wrappers and pinch closed.
3. To fry dumplings, preheat oil for 30 seconds on high heat, then lower heat to medium. Cook dumplings on each side for about 3 minutes or until golden brown.

LEFTOVER CHICKEN AND RICE WITH PINEAPPLE DUMPLINGS

- 1 tsp ginger, microplaned
- 3 Tbsp pineapple juice
- 1 tsp vinegar
- 1 Tbsp soy sauce
- 1 Tbsp cornstarch
- 2 garlic cloves, pressed
- 2 Tbsp oil
- ¼ cup carrot, chopped
- ¼ cup bell pepper (any color), chopped
- ¼ cup pineapple, chopped
- 2 green onions, chopped
- ½ cup cooked rice
- 1 cup leftover cooked chicken, chopped
- 12 dumpling wrappers
- 1 cup of oil for frying
- Thai Sweet Chili Sauce for dipping (see recipe in the Sauces section)

1. In a bowl, combine ginger, pineapple juice, vinegar, soy sauce, cornstarch, and garlic. Set aside.
2. In a wok, heat 2 Tbsp oil. Add carrot, bell pepper, pineapple, and onions. Sauté until veggies are tender. Remove from heat.
3. Toss veggies with rice and chicken. Toss with sauce. Blend well.
4. Spoon mixture into dumpling wrappers and pinch closed.
5. To fry dumplings, preheat oil for 30 seconds on high heat, then lower heat to medium. Cook dumplings on each side for about 3 minutes or until golden brown.
6. Serve hot with Thai Sweet Chili Sauce for dipping.

LEFTOVER PORK, APPLE, AND CHEESE DUMPLINGS

- 1 cup leftover cooked pork, chopped
- ½ cup apple, shopped
- ½ cup cheese, shredded
- 12 dumpling wrappers
- 1 cup of oil for frying

1. Combine pork, apple, and cheese.
2. Spoon mixture into dumpling wrappers and pinch closed.
3. To fry dumplings, preheat oil for 30 seconds on high heat, then lower heat to medium. Cook dumplings on each side for about 3 minutes or until golden brown.

PART III

SWEET DUMPLINGS

CRAB RANGOON

Back when I lived in Missouri, there was a little Chinese restaurant that had the best sweet crab Rangoon. I would eat them as a dessert they were so sweet. I think I have done a pretty good job of recreating them here. The secret is using honey as a sweetener instead of sugar.

- 4 oz cream cheese
- ¼ cup imitation crab meat, chopped (you can use real crab meat, but imitation is slightly sweeter)
- ¼ cup milk
- 1 Tbsp honey
- 12 dumpling wrappers
- 1 cup of oil for frying

1. Mix all filling ingredients together.
2. Spoon mixture into dumpling wrappers and pinch closed.
3. To fry dumplings, preheat oil for 30 seconds on high heat, then lower heat to medium. Cook dumplings on each side for about 3 minutes or until golden brown.

RED BEAN DUMPLINGS

While found in baozi, mooncakes, and other Chinese pastries, red bean paste isn't typically found inside a dumpling wrapper in China, but this dumpling was specifically requested by Joshua Hislop and David Kretz, Kickstarter backers, so why not put it in a dumpling?

- ½ cup dry azuki beans
- lots of water
- ½ cup sugar
- ½ cup oil
- 12 dumpling wrappers
- 1 cup of oil for frying

1. In a large pot, cover the beans in water and soak overnight (at least 8 hours).
2. After soaking, bring beans and water to a boil. Boil for at least 2 hours, continually adding water as necessary (water will boil away), until beans are soft enough to mash with a fork.

3. Drain beans and process in a blender until smooth.
4. In a wok, heat up ½ cup of oil. Add blended beans and sugar. Fry beans on medium-low heat, continually stirring and pressing with a spatula, until dry.
5. Spoon mixture into dumpling wrappers and pinch closed.
6. To fry dumplings, preheat oil for 30 seconds on high heat, then lower heat to medium. Cook dumplings on each side for about 3 minutes or until golden brown.

CHEESECAKE DUMPLINGS

Cheesecake, like dumplings, is very versatile. You can brighten this basic recipe up by drizzling the dumplings with chocolate syrup or you can be really fancy and add the juice of one lemon to the filling and then top the dumplings with strawberry jam. And those are just two ideas! How will you make your cheesecake dumplings unique?

- 4 oz cream cheese, room temperature
- ½ cup sugar
- 1 Tbsp flour
- 1 tsp vanilla
- 1 egg
- 1 egg yolk
- ¼ cup milk
- 12 dumpling wrappers
- 1 cup of oil for frying

1. Mix cream cheese, sugar, flour and vanilla together. Blend thoroughly (can use an electric mixer on medium speed)

2. Add in egg and egg yolk. Blend thoroughly.
3. Add in milk. Blend thoroughly until mixture is smooth.
4. Spoon mixture into dumpling wrappers and pinch closed.
5. To fry dumplings, preheat oil for 30 seconds on high heat, then lower heat to medium. Cook dumplings on each side for about 3 minutes or until golden brown.
6. Always cut a dumpling open to make sure it is cooked through.

BANANA CARAMEL DUMPLINGS

A carnival favorite, adapted as a dumpling.

- 2 Tbsp butter
- 3 Tbsp brown sugar
- 2 bananas, peeled and chopped
- ¼ cup orange juice
- 1 tsp cinnamon, plus more for garnish

1. Melt the butter in a saucepan over low heat.
2. Add the brown sugar and the bananas, stirring gently.
3. Add the orange juice and cinnamon.
4. Mash some of the bananas, but the mixture should remain thick and lumpy. Remove from heat.
5. Let the mixture cool before handling.
6. Spoon mixture into dumpling wrappers and pinch closed.
7. To fry dumplings, preheat oil for 30 seconds on high heat, then lower heat to medium. Cook dumplings on each side for about 3 minutes or until golden brown.

8. Serve hot, dusted with cinnamon.

KEY LIME PIE DUMPLINGS

*As a Floridian, I had to include a key lime pie dumpling. You should not try
to substitute regular limes for key limes. The flavor will not be the same.
Serve these with the Florida Conch Dumplings for a totally Florida dinner!*

- 1 graham cracker, crumbled
- ½ cup freshly squeezed key lime juice
- 2 egg yolks
- ½ can sweetened condensed milk
- ¼ cup sour cream
- 12 dumpling wrappers
- 1 cup of oil for frying
- whipped cream (optional) for topping
- lime zest (optional) for garnish

1. Combine graham cracker, lime juice, egg yolks, milk, and
   sour cream. Mix well with a whisk. Place in the fridge for
   15 minutes to chill so the filling will sit up.
2. Spoon mixture into dumpling wrappers and pinch closed.

3. To fry dumplings, preheat oil for 30 seconds on high heat, then lower heat to medium. Cook dumplings on each side for about 3 minutes or until golden brown.
4. Always cut a dumpling open to make sure it is cooked through.
5. Serve topped with whipped cream and sprinkled with lime zest.

APPLE PIE DUMPLINGS

An all-American favorite adapted as a dumpling. Serve with a scoop of vanilla ice cream to make it a la mode!

- 1 cup apple, chopped
- ¼ cup sugar
- 1 Tbsp flour
- 1 tsp cinnamon
- 1 tsp nutmeg
- 1 tsp lemon juice
- 12 dumpling wrappers
- 1 cup of oil for frying

1. Mix filling ingredients.
2. Spoon mixture into dumpling wrappers and pinch closed.
3. To fry dumplings, preheat oil for 30 seconds on high heat, then lower heat to medium. Cook dumplings on each side for about 3 minutes or until golden brown.

CHERRY PIE DUMPLINGS

Try serving these dumplings a la mode like a proper cherry pie!

- 1 cup cherries, pitted
- ½ cup sugar
- 2 Tbsp cornstarch
- 1 tsp vanilla extract
- 12 dumpling wrappers
- 1 cup of oil for frying

1. In a saucepan, heat cherries over medium heat until they lose their juices, 5-7 minutes. Remove from heat.
2. In another bowl, mix sugar and cornstarch. Add mixture to hot cherries. Add in vanilla extract.
3. Return to stove and simmer over low heat until mixture thickens, stirring continually. Remove from heat and let cool before handling.
4. Spoon mixture into dumpling wrappers and pinch closed.

5. To fry dumplings, preheat oil for 30 seconds on high heat, then lower heat to medium. Cook dumplings on each side for about 3 minutes or until golden brown.

PUMPKIN PIE DUMPLINGS

The perfect finish after the Turkey-Day Leftover Dumplings and the Broccoli Cheese Rice Dumplings. This is a recipe to make the pie filling from scratch because it is healthier and more readily available than canned pumpkin.

- 1 small pumpkin (1 cup pumpkin puree)
- 1/3 cup sugar
- 1 tsp cinnamon powder
- 1 tsp ground cloves
- 1 tsp allspice powder
- ½ tsp ginger powder
- 1 egg
- 6 oz evaporated milk
- ½ teaspoon vanilla extract
- 12 dumpling wrappers
- 1 cup of oil for frying
- whipped cream for topping (technically optional, but who can eat pumpkin pie without whipped topping?)

Preparing the Pumpkin

1. Cut the pumpkin in half and remove the seeds. Don't be afraid to scrape the sides and get all that stringy stuff out.
2. Place the pumpkin in a steamer basket on the stove (you can cut the pieces smaller if they don't quite fit). Steam pumpkin, covered, over high heat for 20-30 minutes or until it is soft.
3. Scoop softened pumpkin meat out of the rind. Puree pumpkin meat in a blender until smooth.
4. Done! You will only need 1 cup of puree for this recipe. If you have extra puree, you can freeze it and save it for future dumplings, make a batch of Vash's Pup Dog Treat Dumplings, or increase the rest of the recipe to make lots of dumplings (not like they will go to waste since they will be eaten up so quickly!).

Making the Dumplings

1. Mix 1 cup of pumpkin puree with the sugar, spices, egg, and evaporated milk.
2. Spoon mixture into dumpling wrappers and pinch closed. If the mixture is too runny to work with, put the mixture into the refrigerator for about 20 minutes to set up.
3. To fry dumplings, preheat oil for 30 seconds on high heat, then lower heat to medium. Cook dumplings on each side for about 3 minutes or until golden brown.
4. Serve topped with whipped cream.

"MINCEMEAT" PIE DUMPLINGS

Originally made with meat, "mincemeat" pies gradually lost their meat, but kept their name. This traditional Christmas dessert is given a new shape and a new presentation as a dumpling.

- ½ cup raisins
- ½ cup apples, chopped
- 2 Tbsp orange juice
- 1 Tbsp apple cider vinegar
- ¼ cup white sugar
- ¼ cup brown sugar
- 1 tsp cinnamon
- 1 tsp nutmeg
- 1 graham cracker, crumbled
- 12 dumpling wrappers
- 1 cup of oil for frying

1. In a saucepan, add raisins, apples, juice, and vinegar.

Cook over medium heat for about 20 minutes or until apple pieces are soft.

2. Stir in sugars, spices, and graham cracker. Remove from heat and let the mixture cool before handling.

3. Spoon mixture into dumpling wrappers and pinch closed.

4. To fry dumplings, preheat oil for 30 seconds on high heat, then lower heat to medium. Cook dumplings on each side for about 3 minutes or until golden brown.

THREE BERRY PIE DUMPLINGS

Kickstarter backer Sarah Green asked for a mixed fruit dumpling. This is an easy, delicious, and impressive dumpling to serve for family and friends.

- ¼ cup sugar
- 1 Tbsp cornstarch
- ½ cup strawberries, chopped
- ½ cup blueberries, roughly mashed
- ½ cup raspberries, roughly mashed
- 12 dumpling wrappers
- 1 cup of oil for frying
- ice cream (optional)
- whipped cream (optional)

1. Mix together sugar and cornstarch. Add in berries and mix well. Let mixture rest for about 15 minutes.
2. Spoon mixture into dumpling wrappers and pinch closed.
3. To fry dumplings, preheat oil for 30 seconds on high heat,

then lower heat to medium. Cook dumplings on each side for about 3 minutes or until golden brown.

4. Serve warm with ice cream or whipped cream.

CINNAMON ROLL DUMPLINGS

I originally made these for a Disney World cooking contest. I didn't win, but neither did anyone else, so at least I didn't lose! Try serving these on a Saturday morning as a yummy breakfast.

- 1 Tbsp butter, softened
- ¼ cup brown sugar
- ½ Tbsp cinnamon powder
- ¼ cup powdered sugar
- 1 Tbsp milk
- 12 dumpling wrappers
- 1 cup of oil for frying

1. Combine butter, brown sugar, and cinnamon. Mix until smooth.
2. Spoon mixture into dumpling wrappers and pinch closed.
3. To fry dumplings, preheat oil for 30 seconds on high heat, then lower heat to medium. Cook dumplings on each side for about 3 minutes or until golden brown.

4. To make the icing, combine powdered sugar and milk. Whisk until smooth. Plate the dumplings and drizzle the icing on top.

CHOCOLATE PUDDING WITH BACON DUMPLINGS

Okay, okay. You don't have to have bacon in this dumpling, but man oh man is it good. My sisters and I have been dipping our bacon into "chocolate gravy" (chocolate pudding) since before bacon was cool. Any Arkansans reading this book will know what I'm talking about. Also, you can try using black cocoa powder in this recipe to make black (super dark) chocolate pudding. Kickstarter backer Amanda Maus really loves pure chocolate, so I think a black chocolate pudding here would fit that bill.

- 2 slices fried, crispy bacon, chopped
- 1 cup of milk, divided
- ¼ cup sugar
- 3 Tbsp cocoa powder
- 2 tsp cornstarch
- dash of salt
- 1 egg yolk
- 1 tsp vanilla extract
- 12 dumpling wrappers
- 1 cup of oil for frying

1. In a saucepan, whisk together ½ cup of milk, sugar, and cocoa. Heat over medium heat until steaming (does not need to boil). Remove from heat.
2. In a bowl, whisk together remaining milk, cornstarch, salt, egg, and vanilla.
3. Slowly drizzle egg mixture into milk mixture, whisking constantly. Heat mixture over medium heat, stirring constantly to prevent burning. Once it starts to boil, cook for about 2 minutes more while mixture thickens. Remove from heat. If the mixture is still a little thin, that is okay; it will thicken as it cools.
4. Mix in bacon. Let mixture sit up for about 15 minutes.
5. Spoon mixture into dumpling wrappers and pinch closed.
6. To fry dumplings, preheat oil for 30 seconds on high heat, then lower heat to medium. Cook dumplings on each side for about 3 minutes or until golden brown.

FRUIT WITH YOGURT HONEY DUMPLINGS

Kickstarter backer Amber McGahey requested a fruit and honey dumpling similar to what her grandmother would make in Hokkaido, Japan. Unfortunately, I wasn't able to find any fruit dumpling recipes specifically related to Hokkaido, but I did find out what fruits are grown there and also learned that the region has a thriving dairy industry. So while this probably isn't exactly what Amber remembers, it's still pretty good!

- ½ cup yogurt
- 1 Tbsp honey
- 1 tsp vanilla extract
- ½ cup apples, chopped
- ½ cup grapes, roughly mashed
- ½ cup peaches, chopped
- 12 dumpling wrappers
- 1 cup of oil for frying

1. In a bowl, combine yogurt, honey, and vanilla. Blend well.

2. Add in fruits. Blend well.
3. Spoon mixture into dumpling wrappers and pinch closed.
4. To fry dumplings, preheat oil for 30 seconds on high heat, then lower heat to medium. Cook dumplings on each side for about 3 minutes or until golden brown.

S'MORES DUMPLINGS

Kickstarter backer, and my wonderful sister-in-law, Delaney Anderson, and my father-in-law Derek requested this dumpling. I only officially included the basic s'mores ingredients in this recipe, but there are lots of ways you can make your s'mores dumplings crazy! Try replacing the chocolate with chopped up or crushed bits of your favorite candy bar. Make chocolate chocolate chocolate s'mores by using chocolate grahams and chocolate marshmallows. Make grasshopper s'mores by using mint chocolate. Add some fruit like strawberry or bananas. Make chocolate peanut butter s'mores by using chocolate grahams and peanut butter instead of chocolate pieces. Use dark or black chocolate for a really rich taste or use chili chocolate for a hit of spice!

- 2 graham crackers, crumbled
- ½ cup of mini marshmallows
- ½ cup mini-chocolate chips
- 12 dumpling wrappers
- 1 cup of oil for frying

1. Combine the graham crackers, marshmallows, and chocolate chips in a bowl.
2. Spoon mixture into dumpling wrappers and pinch closed.
3. To fry dumplings, preheat oil for 30 seconds on high heat, then lower heat to medium. Cook dumplings on each side for about 3 minutes or until golden brown.

BONUS RECIPE! VASH'S PUP DOG TREAT DUMPLINGS

Somehow, my dog knows when I am making dumplings. She always sits attentively by when I cook, but she gets especially excited and nosey when I make dumplings. I'm sure it has nothing to do with the fact that I tend to drop pieces of dumpling wrappers on the floor when shaping them or just toss her ones that break open or are too hideous to salvage. Of course, not all dumpling ingredients are puppy dog safe (pepper, onions, chocolate, and raisins are all unsafe for doggies). And dogs should never eat fried food. These yummy doggie-safe dumplings are best steamed, just make sure they fully cool before giving them to your best little buddy!

½ cup canned pumpkin (or homemade pumpkin puree, see recipe under the Pumpkin Pie Dumpling recipe)

2 Tbsp honey

2 Tbsp water

1 Tbsp vegetable oil

1 cup flour (white flour, whole wheat flour, or oats are all safe for dogs)

1 tsp cinnamon (optional)

12 dumpling wrappers

1. Combine all filling ingredients. Blend well.
2. Spoon mixture into wrappers and pinch closed.
3. To steam dumplings, place in a steamer basket or on an elevated plate in a wok over water on high heat for about 10 minutes.

My sweet Vash, helping me shop for dumpling ingredients.

PART IV

SAUCES

TANGY TOMATO SAUCE

This recipe goes great with the Bison Ball Dumplings, but it's also a good sauce to have on hand to add a kick to lots of foods. Try it instead of regular ketchup on anything you would put ketchup on to take your food to the next level.

- 2 Tbsp dill pickle relish
- ¼ cup ketchup
- 7 oz can of tomato sauce
- 2 Tbsp onion, chopped
- 2 Tbsp brown sugar
- 1 Tbsp Worcestershire sauce
- ¼ cup water
- 1 Tbsp vinegar
- Dash of pepper

1. Add all ingredients together in a saucepan and simmer over medium heat for 15 minutes, stirring constantly.

2. Let sauce cool completely before transferring to an airtight container and refrigerating.

CHINESE CHILI SAUCE

Chinese Chili Sauce is very spicy, so it goes great with mild dumplings, or feel free to pair it with the spicy dumplings in the book if you like to live dangerously.

- 10 dried red chilies
- 1 cup hot water
- 1 garlic clove, pressed
- 2 Tbsp brown sugar
- 1 tsp salt
- 4 Tbsp white vinegar
- 2 Tbsp sesame oil

1. Soak the chilies in hot water for about 20 minutes.
2. Put softened chilies, garlic, sugar, salt, and vinegar into a blender and grind to desired texture. Remove chili paste from blender and set aside.
3. Heat sesame oil in a wok until it starts to smoke. Remove from heat.

4. In a bowl, combine chili paste and sesame oil. Mix well.
5. Let sauce cool completely before transferring to an airtight container and refrigerating.

THAI SWEET CHILI SAUCE

This sauce goes great with so many dumplings, from Traditional Dumplings to Sweet and Sour Chicken Dumplings. This recipe makes a small amount, but feel free to double or triple it to keep a jar around to use with dumplings and lots of other foods that need a sweet and spicy kick.

- 3 garlic cloves, pressed
- 2 red jalapeno or Serrano peppers, seeds removed for less heat
- ¼ cup white distilled vinegar
- ½ cup sugar
- ¾ cup water
- ½ Tbsp salt
- 1 Tbsp cornstarch
- 2 tablespoons water

1. Combine all ingredients in a blender except for cornstarch and water. Puree ingredients.

2. Transfer mixture to a saucepan and bring to a boil over
    medium heat. Simmer mixture until it begins to thicken.
3. In a cup, whisk together cornstarch and water. Whisk
    cornstarch mixture into the chili mixture and simmer
    sauce for one more minute.
4. Let sauce cool completely before transferring to an
    airtight container and refrigerating.

MARINARA SAUCE

As I mentioned earlier, I was very proud the first time I made spaghetti sauce from scratch. This recipe makes enough sauce for a batch of dumplings, but you can easily double this recipe and add a pound of ground beef to make a full pot of spaghetti sauce.

- 4 large tomatoes, peeled and seeds removed
- ¼ cup onion, chopped
- ¼ cup mushrooms, chopped
- ¼ cup green bell pepper, chopped
- 1 garlic clove, pressed
- 1 Tbsp Italian seasoning
- 1 tsp salt

1. Pulse tomatoes in a blender until smooth.
2. In a large saucepan, add all ingredients. Bring to a boil, then reduce heat and simmer for at least 20 minutes. The sauce should reduce and darken. It might take a bit longer, depending on the quality of the tomatoes.

3. Remove from heat and serve hot. Let leftover sauce cool completely before transferring to an airtight container and refrigerating.

BUFFALO SAUCE

This is a traditional Buffalo Sauce, but for the Buffalo Chicken Dumplings, feel free to use any wing sauce you want to make them your own.

- 3 Tbsp butter
- 4 Tbsp Tabasco sauce
- 1 Tbsp paprika
- ½ tsp salt
- ½ tsp cayenne pepper
- ¼ tsp black pepper

1. In a small saucepan, melt butter.
2. After butter is melted, add all the other ingredients. Gently bring to a boil.
3. Remove from heat. Let cool before transferring to an airtight container and refrigerating.

SWEET AND SOUR SAUCE

This sauce is perfect for Sweet and Sour Dumplings, and it uses a lot less sugar than commercial sauces.

- ½ cup pineapple juice
- 3 Tbsp light brown sugar
- 3 Tbsp apple cider vinegar
- ¼ cup chicken stock
- 4 tsp cornstarch
- 4 tsp water

1. Mix all ingredients together except for cornstarch and water. Bring to a boil. Reduce heat and let sauce simmer for about 5 minutes.
2. In a bowl, whisk together cornstarch and water. Slowly add cornstarch mix to pineapple sauce, whisking

continually. Continue to let sauce simmer until thickened to desired consistency.

3. Remove from heat. Let cool before transferring to an airtight container and refrigerating.

SALSA

Of course, it is easy and cheap to buy a jar of salsa in most Western countries, but in China, it is expensive and can be difficult to find. But even if you live in the West, try using this easy recipe for a small amount of homemade salsa! It's always better to cook local and organic when you can, so give it a try. Also, if you just finely chop and mix the ingredients but don't cook them, you'll have a delicious pico de gallo.

- 6 medium-sized tomatoes (~2 pounds worth), peeled, seeds removed, chopped
- 1 onion, chopped
- 2 garlic cloves, pressed
- 2 Tbsp fresh cilantro, chopped
- juice of 1 lemon
- ¼ tsp oregano
- 1 green bell pepper, chopped
- 1 tap black pepper
- Salt to taste
- 1 jalapeño, chopped, seeds removed for less heat

1. Put all the ingredients in a saucepan and gently bring to a simmer.
2. Taste mixture as it cooks. Add salt and jalapeño seeds to taste.
3. Remove from heat when salsa reaches desired taste/consistency.
4. Salsa can keep for about 4 weeks in the refrigerator. Let it cool before transferring to an airtight container and refrigerating.

GUACAMOLE

Guacamole may be one of the most delicious things on the whole planet. When I first moved to China, I went through guacamole withdrawal because I couldn't get avocados in my tiny town, but now, you can find avocados everywhere! Delicious and easy to make, there is never a reason to buy prepared guacamole at a supermarket or import store!

- 2 ripe avocados
- 1 tomato, peeled, seeds removed, chopped
- ¼ cup onion, chopped
- Juice of 1 lime
- 1 garlic clove, pressed
- 2 Tbsp fresh cilantro, chopped (or as much as you want. I like a LOT!)

1. Slice open avocados and spoon out meat. Using a fork and a spoon, mash the avocado meat.
2. Add remaining ingredients and blend thoroughly.

3. Serve and eat within 24 hours. Guacamole does not keep well for much longer than a day.

STRAWBERRY ONION JAM

This fun sauce is a perfect partner for the rich, savoriness of the mock foie gras dumplings.

- 1 Tbsp oil
- 1 onion, chopped
- 10 oz strawberry jam
- juice of 1 lemon

1. In a wok, heat oil. Add onion and sauté for about 2 minutes or until golden brown.
2. In a blender, add cooked onion, strawberry jam, and lemon juice. Pulse until smooth.
3. Transfer mixture to an airtight container and refrigerate.

TARTAR SAUCE

I add cilantro to my Tartar Sauce for an extra kick of flavor. Try it with all your fish-based dishes.

- 1 cup plain yogurt
- Juice of 1 lemon
- 2 Tbsp cilantro, chopped
- 2 green onions, chopped
- Dash of salt
- Dash of pepper

1. Combine all ingredients.
2. Transfer to an airtight container and refrigerate.

PART V

METRIC CONVERSIONS

One of the biggest issues with being an American trying to cook in China is the metric conversions, so I've included this handy chart to help you adapt the recipes to however you are comfortable.

VOLUME CONVERSIONS

U.S. Volume Measure	Metric Equivalent
1/8 teaspoon	0.5 milliliters
¼ teaspoon	1 milliliter
½ teaspoon	2 milliliters
1 teaspoon	5 milliliters
½ tablespoon	7 milliliters
1 tablespoon (3 teaspoons)	15 milliliters
2 tablespoons (1 fluid ounce)	30 milliliters
¼ cup (4 tablespoons)	60 milliliters
1/3 cup	90 milliliters
½ cup (4 fluid ounces)	125 milliliters
2/3 cup	160 milliliters
¾ cup (6 fluid ounces)	180 milliliters
1 cup (16 tablespoons)	250 milliliters
1 pint (2 cups)	500 milliliters
1 quart (4 CUPS)	1 liter

WEIGHT CONVERSIONS

U.S. Weight Measure	Metric Equivalent
½ ounce	15 grams
1 ounce	30 grams
2 ounce	60 grams
3 ounce	85 grams
¼ pound (4 ounces)	115 grams
½ pound (8 ounces)	225 grams
¾ pound (12 ounces)	340 grams
1 pound (16 ounces)	454 grams

OVEN TEMPERATURE CONVERSIONS

Degrees Fahrenheit	Degrees Celsius
200 degrees F	95 degrees C
250 degrees F	120 degrees C
275 degrees F	135 degrees C
300 degrees F	150 degrees C
325 degrees F	160 degrees C
350 degrees F	180 degrees C
375 degrees F	190 degrees C
400 degrees F	205 degrees C
425 degrees F	220 degrees C
450 degrees F	230 degrees C

ABOUT THE AUTHOR

Amanda Roberts is a USA Today bestselling author who has been living in China since 2010. She has an MA in English from the University of Central Missouri and has been published in magazines, newspapers, and anthologies around the world. Amanda can be found all over the Internet, but her home is AmandaRobertsWrites.com.

Website: http://amandarobertswrites.com/
Newsletter: http://amandarobertswrites.com/subscribe-crazy-dumplings/
Facebook: https://www.facebook.com/AmandaRobertsWrites/
Instagram: https://www.instagram.com/amandarobertswrites/
Goodreads: https://www.goodreads.com/Amanda_Roberts
BookBub: https://www.bookbub.com/authors/amanda-roberts-2bfe99dd-ea16-4614-a696-84116326dcd1
Email: Amanda@AmandaRobertsWrites.com

THANK YOU!

This book would not have been possible without the hundreds of people who supported it on Kickstarter! Thank you to the craziest backers on the planet! The names in bold are people who donated at least $40 and are my extra crazy backers.

A Jacob Cord

Aaron Beard

Aaron Bretveld

Aaron White

abitha!

AC

Adrienne Hood

Agos

Aimee Yermish

Aleta Johansen

Alex "Dumpling" Devine

alex chinchilla

Alexandra Hayes

Alexandra Pierce

Alison Benowitz

Alison Guthrie

Alistair

Allison Ko

Amanda Lucas

Amazinmic

Amber E

Amber McGahey

Amelia Hite

Amy Bolaa

Amy Hart

Anand Patel

Andreas Burman

Andrew Eden-Balfour

Andrew Heley

Andrew Sinsbury

Andy

Angela Chatha

Angela Efros

Angela Green

Angela Pritchett

Angie Doan

Ann Foerster

Anna Carmona

Anne O'Hehir

AP

Archer Family

Aya Nissan

Balázs Kosaras

Ben H

Ben Shultz

Bernard De Santis III

Beth Domann

Beth Krumholz

Bill Reuther

Brad Cook

Brad Scanlan

Brandon Inoue

Breanna Gallagher

Brian & Lee Roberson

Brian and Emily

Brian S. Weddle

Brittany Inglese

Brittany Miller

Bryce Marley

Bryce O

C Asuncion

C J Ihre

Cambear

Cameron Calka

Camey Johnson

Candace Fetzer

Carb Freedom - www.carbfreedom.com

Carl Coates

Carl L Gilchrist

Carla Castillo

Carlos Balthazar

Carlos Díez

Carol Schutte

Carolyn Brindle

Catherine Brown

Chad Essmam

Charis

Charlie Prince

Charlsie Evans

Cherith Yosef

Chris E

Chris Edwards

Chris Hardham

Christian Wirtz

Christine Venart

Cindy Kommerkamp

Claire Lewis

Coreen Battiato

Dan

Dan Canzonieri

Dan Cooke

Dana Laskowski

Dane Evans

Daniel Freytes

Daniel Haas

Daniel Lanigan

Danielle Greene

Davi Figueiredo

David A.Singer

David Donovan & Liu Nanxue

David Kretz

David Spaxman

Dawn Marie

Deb "Seattlejo" Schumacher

Deirdre Morrison

Denise Newton

Derek

Diane W Coombs

Donna Nutter

dsiewert

Duncan Stockwell

Dwight Bisho

E. Gottlieb

Eileen Hendriksen

Eileen LaBoone

Elise van Os

Eleanor Erwin

Elisabeth Allen

Emma W-B

Eric and Lauren Horbinski

Eric Damon Walters

Eric Schaffer

Eric Tuennecke

Erica Creighton

Erik Singer

Evan Eyster

Familjen Silvstål

Florian Tischner

Florijn Terstal

Frank Laycock

Gail

Gareth Shelton

Gaston Prudon

Geoff Peterson

Ginai Cuyugan

grace green

Guy deWardener

H J

Hannah

Hans K

Heather Blandford

Heather L. Whittaker

Helen Christie

Helen Luan

Helena Chestnut

henrik svedros piironen

Holden Landon Austin Phipps

Holly

In memoriam: Eugenia S. Green

In Memory of Ridley Mateo Censon

Ivan Sanchez

J David Warren

J.

J. Thomas

Jack Jenkins

Jack Oskay

Jacob Thomas Burley

James "Peking Duck" McKendrew

James K. Tinsley, Jr.

James Yuen

Jan De Bondt

Jan L.

Jasmine Fellows

Jason and Aimee Spoerlein

Jason Reid

Jason Tubbs

Jay Haney

Jayme McLeish

JB3

Jeffrey Hartnett

Jeffrey Pye

Jennifer Clark

Jennifer Collins

Jennifer Lake

Jeremy Krantz

Jerome "Dim Sum" Lim

Jerry Walter

Jess Wright

Jesse Worsham

Jessica Kilgore

Jia & Greg

Jim Kaucher

Jimbo Michels

Jo Summers

Joe Seliga

Johan Carlsson

John Ewen

John Gillespie

John Gulezian

Johnathon Opstad

Jon P.

Jonas Claumarch

Jonathan Edwards

Jonathan Turpie

Jonathon Powell

Jory Bernstein

Joseph Moyer

Joshua B Marin

Joshua Hislop

JR

Juan Verdickt

Justin Baldock

Justin Barber

Justin Poh

Justin Varney

Juurd ketting

Kalkail

Kalli

Kara Finley

Karen Barnard

Kari Rocha de Martinez

Karla Darrell

Kate Lindinger

Kate Scott

Katharine

Kathi

Kathleen Doerr

Kathy Mayeda

Katie

Katie Stillman

Kay

Keith Solomon

Kelly DeSando

Kent Keltner

Kerri Miller

Kevin homann

Kevin Kolodziej

Kieran "King of the Dumplings" Hanna

Kim Dyer

Kim Zenizo

Kirsten Zaki

Kit Wickliff

Korey

Kristin LaRoche

Kristine Harwood

Kristopher Stein

Kristy Wheeldon

Kyle Turner

Laura Buschelmann

Laura Lundy

Lauren Pitz

Laurent & Noi

Leann Johnson

Lee Waters

Leela Giannasi

Leigh Anne Vanhoozer

Lenaldo Rocha

Leona Gregory

Liam Nolosco

Liam Williams

Lisa Bagwell

Liz Chai

Lizzie Hudson

Louise Williams

Luke Eperthener

Luke Knight

Luke Otlang

Madi

Marc Taylor

Marc Wydler

Marcus Law

Margaret Sherman

Margaret St. John

Margitta Zwyer

Marijo Yates

Mark Cleary

Mark Henderson

Mark M Slocum

Matt Morgan

Matt Tolle

Matt Zaba

Matthew Fochs

Maureen Vaughan

Max Preusse

Max Zomborszki

美格

Melanie Schmidt

Melina Krönert

Michael Armey

Michael Brand

Michael Court

Michael Hughes-Narborough

Michael M. Kroeker

Michael M. Pieler

Michael Michelini

Michael Otto

Michael R. Ward

Michael Salter

Michael Wick

Michelle Parrinello-Cason

Mig Carbonell

Mike F.

Mike Gentz

Mike Puente Jr.

Mila

Miranda Coffey

M'lissa Wetherell-Moore

Monkey King

Moonytiger

Mr Conny Paraniak

My wonderful sister-in-law

Myers

Nannaya Jampala

Natalia Woolhouse

Natasha Bennett

Nathan Miller

Neil Graham

Nicholas Smillie

Nick

Nick & Megan NOLA

Nicole Lavallee

Nirven

Nova C

Oliver J

Patrick Fletcher

PatrickW

Paul Kuperman

Paul novak

Paul Sudlow

Paula F.

Peter Warnock

Peter & Terri

Ramin Sabzbalouch

Randi Breivik

Rebecca Dixon

René Hjorth

Richard en Chikmah Schutte

Richard Fusco

Rilla Websdale

Rob Coke

Rob McKeagney

Rob Steinberger

Robert Alan Harris III

Robert Gunn

Robert Rauch

Robert Suizu

Rodrigo Perez

Roger Tjosås

Rudy "Chainsaw" Basso

Ryan Handberg

Ryan McCormick Wheel Price, Esq.

Sam White

Samantha Sayuri Matsumoto Casillas

Sarah Behling

Sarah Chen

Sarah DeBaar

Sayaka Osawa

Schiltz G.

Scott

Scott Hill

Scott Loonan

Shaheena Khan

Shannon Hutchinson

Shannon Sailer

Sharon Nissen

Shean, Semeicha and Sapphira Mohammed

ShenzhenParty.com

Shirley Tseng

Shoually Stahr

Simon Harkins

Siobhan Archer-Morris

Sondre Nilsen

Sonja

Soo Kuan

Stacy

Stefan Winkler

Steffen Heise

Stephanie Gonzales

Stephanie Osta-Burman

Stephen Mark Lato

Stephenie Cheng-LaBoyne

Steve Cullity

Steve Eckart

Steve Korchmar

Steve Proctor

Steve Waddell

Steve Yao

Stijn Hommes

Stuart Satterfield

Sunny

Suzanne St Thomas

Sven Böyng

T Laws

Ted Beyer

Tek Shen Ling

Tessa & Garrett

The Burns Family

The Cleaver Quarterly

Theo Murphy

Thierry Corlieto

Thomas Lippert

Tim Parker-Smith

Tom

Tom Anderson, Newport Beach

Tomas Denemark

Tony Shum

Tory S

Toyon

Travis J. Hansen

Tristan Colson

Tyler Chorneyko

Vic Eichhorn

Vincent B. Donadio

William Collins

William Donovan

William Hall

www.headheartandtail.com

Yonatan

Zach

Zach Bledsoe

Zachary Brumleve

Zachary Hany

Zemma Charles

Zhu Xiao Dong

Zita Haglund

www.ingramcontent.com/pod-product-compliance
Lightning Source LLC
Chambersburg PA
CBHW071406150726
48000CB00001B/188